PARTNERS TO HISTORY

Martin Luther King Jr., Ralph David Abernathy, and the Civil Rights Movement

PARTNERS TO HISTORY

Martin Luther King Jr., Ralph David Abernathy, and the Civil Rights Movement

By DONZALEIGH ABERNATHY

Foreword by Robert F. Kennedy Jr.

Crown Publishers
New York

Published by Crown Publishers, New York, New York.
Member of the Crown Publishing Group, a division of
Random House, Inc.
www.randomhouse.com

CROWN is a trademark and the Crown colophon is a
registered trademark of Random House, Inc.

Printed in Singapore

Design by Susan Landesmann Design

Library of Congress Cataloging-in-Publication Data

Abernathy, Donzaleigh.
  Partners to history: Martin Luther King Jr., Ralph David
Abernathy, and the civil rights movement / by Donzaleigh Abernathy;
foreword by Robert F. Kennedy Jr.
    p.   cm.
  Includes bibliographical references and index.
  1. African Americans—Civil rights—History—20th century. 2. Civil
rights movements—United States—History—20th century. 3. King,
Martin Luther, Jr., 1929–1968. 4. Abernathy, Ralph, 1926–1990   .
5. African American civil rights workers—Biography. I. Title.
E185.61.A165   2002
323.1′196073—dc21   2001047564
                                                CIP

ISBN 0-609-60914-9

10 9 8 7 6 5 4 3 2 1

First Edition

For the children: Ralph IV, Christiana, Micah, Alexander, Sören-Niklas,
and those to be born

To My Parents

Mother . . .
A fine lady anchored in Christian love
For loving Daddy, and for being a great mom.
For always placing us first.
For giving us quality, the classics,
  and the finest education.
For taking us as a family on every
  major civil rights march and event.
For housing, teaching, and feeding
  all those movement workers.
For enduring the endless battles
  of the movement—the violence,
  the daily, racist, obscene phone calls,
  the hate mail.
For standing beside Daddy to the end,
  when all you ever wanted was
  a private, simple life.
For giving birth to me and making
  me a woman.

Daddy . . .
My friend, my pastor, my mentor
For loving God.
For loving Mother, and for loving Martin.
For having the courage to do
  what was right.
For improving the quality of life
  for all people of America.
For standing up for truth, justice,
  and equality.
For helping to change the course
  of history.
For the laughter, legacy, and joy.
For your gentle, humble, kind, honest,
  forgiving spirit that never wavered.
For loving your enemies and blessing
  those who persecuted you.
For trying and giving your all.
For gracing us with your presence.

Thank you for loving, accepting, understanding, and teaching me to be the best Donzaleigh that I can be.

Eternally my gratitude and love

CONTENTS

FOREWORD

I grew up in Virginia, so I have my own dim recollections of the injustice of Jim Crow. I've spent much time in the South writing about the Civil Rights Movement, so I have some idea about what it must have been like for Martin Luther King and Ralph David Abernathy during the time their political sensibilities were formed.

When I was a boy, I often rode in a station wagon pulling a horse trailer across Virginia and Maryland to hunts and horse shows with my family groom, a black man named Bill Shamwell, a proud World War II veteran who stood 6'3" and whom I recall for his tremendous physical strength and natural dignity. When we stopped for meals, he gave me money and I went into a roadside restaurant to buy our food. We ate together in the car. I only understood years later why it had to be that way.

At that time, this nation was almost 200 years old, yet democracy was available only to the few. If you were a black in any one of a dozen Southern states in 1961 you had no more rights and no more protection of the law than did a black in South Africa under the system of apartheid.

Every aspect of civil conduct was governed by considerations of race: a black's birth certificate identified him by race; he lived on a segregated street and played in segregated parks and playgrounds; he attended segregated schools; his workplace, restaurants, rest rooms, public transportation, and dance halls and movie theaters were all segregated; he could not marry outside his race; prisons and institutions for the blind and deaf were segregated; his death certificate identified him by race; and he was buried in a segregated cemetery.

The imposition of second-class citizenship on an entire race of American citizens was maintained and enforced through a system of official corruption designed to deprive black citizens of their right to vote. Lowndes County, Alabama— where I lived for almost a year researching a book on the Civil Rights Movement—was, in the early 1960s, one of a dozen or more counties spread across several southern states with a majority of black citizens, yet not a single black voter.

The most heroic aspect of Dr. King's leadership to me was his unflagging devotion to the democratic system. My father's love for democracy was more predictable coming as he did from a political family and the race of Irish immigrants that had flourished under the American political system. But Dr. King's devotion was extraordinary because he grew up in a system that held out the promises of democracy and at the same time denied its privileges and vestiges and protections to his entire race.

During King's lifetime, and as a direct result of his sacrifice and leadership, our nation became a true constitutional democracy for the first time in its history. In fact, the struggle for democracy was the goal for which he sacrificed his life! In this sense, Dr. King, Dr. Abernathy, and the other leaders of the Civil Rights Movement were as much American heroes as any of the authors of the U.S. Constitution or any of those brave Americans who died for our nation during the American Revolution. They completed our democracy. King is one of the many you will meet in this book who gave their hearts, their health, their physical and financial welfare, and sometimes their lives to this noble endeavor.

Dr. King's great wisdom came from his recognition that with the privileges and protection of democracy came individual responsibilities. Primary among those is the duty to obey the law and to vote. He knew that for people to be good citizens they must know both how to rule and to be ruled.

He enlarged on the philosophy of civil disobedience that distinguishes between just laws and unjust laws, stressing the duty to openly and nonviolently disobey unjust laws—those that unfairly limit the reach of democracy (and to be willing to go to jail for the disobedience)—and at the same time he stressed the absolute duty to obey all other laws. He was often criticized for this by contemporaries who saw the whole society as corrupt.

The astounding thing about the Movement is how those who had been so abused by the legal system embraced it so fervently. It was the belief and the moral courage demonstrated by many of the leaders of the Civil Rights Movement to live this philosophy that gave the Movement such appeal to Americans of other races. There is no better story than the Selma march to illustrate their capacity for moral courage.

On Sunday, March 7, 1965, a few hundred followers of King and Abernathy, attempting to march from Selma to Montgomery, were turned back at the Edmund Pettus Bridge by Sheriff Jim Clark and the Dallas County deputies using whips and hoses. King called for national support for a second march the following Tuesday. In response, during the next two days tens of thousands of people arrived in Selma from across the country. On Monday, King requested a federal injunction enjoining Jim Clark from interfering with the marchers. The judge said he was inclined to grant the injunction, but he first wanted to hear from the other side and enjoined King and his followers from marching until that hearing could be held on Wednesday. This was bad news for King, who believed strongly in the rule of law but who already had committed thousands of people to march on Tuesday. His followers and most other civil rights leaders urged him to ignore the federal order.

On Tuesday, thousands of civil rights activists filled the streets of Selma. King and Abernathy led the marchers over the Edmund Pettus Bridge. When they got to the other side—to the scene of the conflict of Bloody Sunday—the same Dallas County possemen and state troopers were waiting. But this time they backed off, opening the road to let King pass, knowing that the marchers would be violating federal law. King's followers were elated to see the open passage and pushed to hurry through, but King stopped at the foot of the bridge and asked the marchers to kneel in prayer. When Abernathy's prayer was completed, King turned and walked through the marchers back across the bridge into Selma. At the top of the bridge he looked back and saw they were following. He prayed again silently in gratitude and relief.

I love this story because it illustrates King's strong belief in the importance of an individual's responsibility to obey and uphold the law in a free society. King was so committed to the concept that he was willing to walk away from his own followers and the Movement that had brought him to power. Perhaps because he had to fight so hard to earn it, Dr. King never took our democracy for granted. He knew that if the rule of law collapsed, the first casualties would be society's weakest and most vulnerable members. He saw, at the end of lawlessness, a lynch mob.

Throughout this book, there are many poignant photos depicting the extraordinary acts of physical courage and the ordinary people who were the soldiers of the Civil Rights Movement. But the book also captures those pivotal moments of moral courage by the Movement's leaders: Dr. King, Dr. Abernathy, and others. Their discipline, restraint, composure, and grace in times of enormous pressure melded these individual acts of bravery into a movement that brought down the mighty walls of oppression and resistance and finally completed our American democracy.

Robert F. Kennedy Jr.

INTRODUCTION

A charge to keep I have;
A God to glorify
Who gave his son my soul to save,
And fit it for the sky.
To serve the present age,
My calling to fulfill;
Oh may it all my powers engage
To do my Master's will.

—A hymn by Charles Wesley

Words can little describe the magnitude of the American Civil Rights Movement—the spirit, the courage of a people, the sacrifices, the joys, the suffering—nor the lives who endured and created these incredibly extraordinary events. In *Partners to History*, I will try to graciously honor those unique individuals who gave of their lives and championed the fight for human rights. I will simply tell you their story, then paint for you with pictures the images and memories of the lives and experiences that I was blessed to share as a child.

When I was little, life was not ordinary as with other children, but for me it was ordinary because it was my life. I was born Donzaleigh Avis in the midst of the August summer heat of the Civil Rights Movement to Ralph David and Juanita Odessa Jones Abernathy. They met when my mother was 16 and married when she turned 21, after Ralph became the pastor of the historic First Baptist Church of Montgomery. He was her first and only love, and that love would last until his death. Their first child, Ralph Jr., died of crib death shortly after birth. Therefore, the arrival of their second child, Juandalynn Ralpheda, gave much comfort to a grief-stricken Juanita.

In 1955, after the arrest of Rosa Parks, my father and his closest friend, Martin Luther King Jr., founded the American Civil Rights Movement. They set into motion the nonviolent struggle for human dignity that would change the course of American history forever. These were the days of segregation and the threat of death was ever present. Just after the success of the Montgomery bus boycott, the fate of Juanita and Juandalynn would be tested with the bombing of our home. These were trying days for my parents and an otherwise dramatic beginning for me. As the third child, my unintended conception occurred from the comfort they sought in each other during those turbulent days.

I don't remember the first time that I met Martin Luther King. I was merely a growth in my mother's stomach. I believe he loved me from the very beginning and that he grew to love me more. He was simply "Uncle Martin"—the giver of love, laughter, happiness, and friendship. Yet, to millions, he was the prophet of an age.

As the first generation of our family to be born in a hospital, our births were attended to by the Catholic nuns of St. Jude Hospital, the only hospital for people of color in Montgomery.

A little over a year later, their fourth child, Ralph David III, was born. Ether was placed on his head accidentally, nearly killing him, to halt his birth until the doctor arrived. Nonetheless, Ralph III would be born strong and determined. It wasn't until July 3, 1971, that Juanita would give birth to their fifth child, Kwame Luthuli, named for Nobel laureate Kwame Nkrumah and Chief Albert Luthuli. Nothing gave us more joy than the birth of Kwame. He represented a new beginning from the tragic end of our lives with Uncle Martin.

As early as I can remember, my father was everything to me. He wrote in his journal that since the student demonstrations had started in Montgomery, he had had only a few hours of sleep a night. His rest was interrupted by the unfriendly telephone calls in the wee hours of the morning, the newspaper drop at 3:00 or 4:00 A.M., the cry of my brother for his bottle, and the daily 5:30 A.M. argument of his daughters over who would get to kiss Daddy first that morning. The sound of little voices made it clear to him "that the night had passed and gone, and that another day with its problems was at hand," which was first posed by his daughters, "who detested eating!" In between breaks of the *Today* show, he wrote that he would try and convince us to wait until Mother awakened later to make us breakfast. "Mother will only give us grits, bacon, milk, eggs, and toast. Or even worse, she might give us oatmeal, and who wants to eat that? What about you making us some sugar pop flakes? These are alright, 'cause Popeye says so on TV." He wrote that we pleaded, "Even if Mother gives us sugar pop flakes, she will not put in enough like you will . . . we think Daddy ought to serve breakfast instead of Mother—you know how to make sugar pop flakes taste so good. Please give us some now." He wrote that we were a "chip off the old block," so he most often would yield because he could not resist, though he vowed not to give in again. "My daughters would forgive me and say, 'See you tomorrow, same time, same station.'"

Daddy brought excitement to our lives and taught us all by his example that courage, strength, patience, humor, and love were needed to live each day to the fullest. He asked me to dream: "Dream big, then make those dreams reality." Often he quoted, "If you cannot be a tree, then be a bush. And if you cannot be a bush, then be a shrub, but be the best little shrub by the side of the road." Before I could read, he had taught me Polonius's advice to Laertes from Shakespeare's *Hamlet*, which included, "To thine ownself be true and it shall follow as the night, the day thou canst not be false to any man." I learned Kipling, Wordsworth, Longfellow, and Thoreau on our weekend excursions with Daddy. His office at our home was my library, my haven and refuge from our public lives. It contained the great books of the Western world: two sets of Britannica encyclopedias; a World Book Encyclopedia for the children; classic literary novels; books of philosophy, religion, sociology, mathematics, poetry, and art. He was always away Monday through Friday on the road with Martin. But he taught us that what he was doing was important, and that we too had to do our part. With love and kindness he guided us, made nonviolence a way of life for us, opened our home to people of all different races and nationalities, and, above all, taught us about God.

He was my father, but he was also my pastor. He said that we were all brothers, all equal in the eyes of God. "Do you think that God loves us more because we are Christian than our brothers who are Muslim, Hindu, Jewish, or Native American? No. We may belong to different faiths but we all serve the same God, the maker of Heaven, earth, and the universe." With those words he opened our minds and our hearts. He taught us to love everyone because God loves them. It is easy to hate, to become embittered with anger, but it takes strength and courage to love.

Partners to History is the story of my father, his best friend, Martin Luther King Jr., and the people he loved, which began long before I was born.

My father's grandfather George was born a slave on a plantation in South Carolina. As a young child, he was auctioned off and taken to live on the Abernathy farm in Linden, Alabama. As the "property" of Mr. Abernathy, George was given his surname and served as a houseworker and playmate for Mr. Abernathy's daughter until he was freed at the age of 12, on January 1, 1863, when President Abraham Lincoln signed the Emancipation Proclamation abolishing slavery in the Southern states. George continued to make Linden his home, where he married Manerva and raised several children. His son, my grandfather Will, a cotton farmer, married Louivery Valentine Bell and purchased over 350 acres of land.

On March 11, 1926, my father, David, was born on his papa's farm in Linden. David was the tenth child of Louivery and

W.L. delivered by her mother, Elen Bell, the midwife for all the black and white children born around Linden back then. Little David used to sit on the porch and shuck peas with Mama, while she sang hymns and talked about the Bible. He would have to carry water to his brothers and sisters in the cotton fields, who weren't too happy that David remained in the shade talking to Mama about God. David said that he met God in a meadow one day and decided to be a preacher of God's word. My aunt Louvenia said he used to preach to the chickens and roosters to make them crow. Grandpa George, a great storyteller, lived long enough to teach David about slavery and Reconstruction, when blacks served in the U.S. Congress and the state legislature, and could exercise their legal right to vote. David's father and Grandpa longed for the day to return when blacks in the South would have the pleasure of voting again. Unable to ever vote, David's papa always told him that "the bottom rail would come to the top," and that "justice would not always be denied to the colored man." David believed in his heart that he could do anything he wanted, and he wanted more than anything to make the world a better place. He staged his first demonstration to protest the inferior science department at his school, Linden Academy, and later, as president of the Student Council of Alabama State, led a hunger strike for improved food and more courteous service. Just before he was drafted into World War II, his sister Manerva added Ralph to his name. Discharged for rheumatic fever, he enrolled at Alabama State College under the G.I. Bill. He majored in mathematics and sociology, and later became a teacher at that college.

In the late 1940s, while earning his master's degree at Atlanta University, Daddy met Martin Luther King Jr. As a young minister, he was in the habit of visiting churches to hear other preachers. On one such visit, to Ebenezer Baptist Church, he was impressed by the oratorical skills of young Martin, an undergraduate of Morehouse College. They spoke briefly and went their separate ways, until a few months later, when Ralph's date stood him up for an evening with Martin. My father was seldom in the habit of abandoning his plans, so he went alone that night to the concert in the chapel at Spellman College. Arriving early, he spotted Martin under a willowy tree. He went over to him to talk about the church only to discover his "date" trying to hide behind the tree. They laughed, and went to the concert together.

They wouldn't meet again until 1950, when Ralph David was serving as young pastor of the historic First Baptist Church of Montgomery.

I have written this book to document in photographs the history of the struggle for civil rights in America. It is said that "a people who do not know their past are destined to repeat it." Far too many sacrifices were made for our freedom to let history repeat itself. It is for these peaceful warriors, the soldiers of freedom, that I pause to remember the road that brought us all across.

Donzaleigh Abernathy

PARTNERS TO HISTORY

Martin Luther King Jr., Ralph David Abernathy, and the Civil Rights Movement

1619
Stolen from Native Shores

We can not dedicate—we can not consecrate—
we can not hallow—this ground. The brave men,
living and dead, who struggled here have conse-
crated it. . . . The world will little note, nor long
remember, what we say here, but it can never
forget what they did here. It is for us the living,
rather, to be dedicated here to the unfinished
work which they who fought here have thus far
so nobly advanced. It is rather for us to be dedicated to the great task remaining before us—
that from these honored dead we take increased
devotion to that cause for which they gave the
last full measure of devotion—that we here
highly resolve that these dead shall not have
died in vain—that this nation, under God, shall
have a new birth of freedom—and that government of the people, by the people, for the people, shall not perish from the earth.

—Abraham Lincoln
The Gettysburg Address, 1863

In August of the year 1619, the first ship carrying African slaves arrived in the port of the Jamestown colony at the mouth of the James River in Virginia. The slaves were to be the free labor force for harvesting the profitable tobacco crop. The African slave was not permitted to assimilate into the white culture, making the color of his skin a "badge of servitude." It was nearly impossible for the African slave to escape back to Africa. Until the further development of America and Canada, the African slave had nowhere to go or hide from the slave owners.

Slave laborers were able to survive and make considerable financial profits for the plantation owners, whereas white indentured servants perished, causing a financial loss. At the end of the Colonial period in American history, the Negro numbered between 400,000 to 500,000 slaves in the colonies. Three-fourths of the African slave population resided in the Southern colonies, where they made up two-fifths of the entire population. It was recorded in South Carolina that African slaves outnumbered the whites two to one. The plantation region consisted of Virginia, Maryland, the Carolinas, and the remaining Southern colonies. These lands were flat, wide coastal plains with spacious bays and harbors and widely navigable rivers. The fertile soil near the banks of the rivers created rich agriculture. Because the tidewater swept up the river, the coast regions came to be known as the tidewater area. Tobacco was the staple crop of the tidewater region. In the Carolinas, rice and indigo were the crops and in the Deep South, or "the black belt" as it would come to be called, cotton would become king.

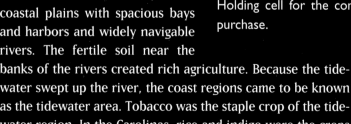

Holding cell for the confinement of slaves prior to purchase.

In the Deep South, where the crop was cotton, the demand for slave labor was insatiable. Eli Whitney's invention of the cotton gin turned the South into the "Cotton Kingdom." Before the Civil War, one-half of the American goods shipped abroad was cotton. It has been recorded that between 1820 and 1860 the number of slaves grew from 1 million to almost 4 million. The price of a slave who worked the fields simultaneously increased from between $300 and $400 to $1,000 and up. The average Southern white family held one to four slaves and at the time of the Civil War an estimated 400,000 Southern white families had slaves. In some cases, if the land holdings were in the tens of thousands of acres, then the slave holdings were in the thousands as well. An average number of slaves on a large plantation ranged from six to seven thousand. With the growing demand for slaves, the great danger for freed slaves was the possibility of being kidnapped and sold back into slavery. Poor white men looked forward to becoming slave owners and the owners of a few slaves longed to become owners of many, while the wealthy landowner's rank in Southern society was determined by the number of human slaves he owned. Slavery of black people was justified by some because black people were not Christians and therefore considered savage. The U.S. Constitution in deciding the appropriations of congressional seats from the South decided in the "Great Compromise" to regard a black person as three-fifths of a human being.

Within the boundaries of the plantation consisted a little village. The owner, his wife, and their family usually lived lavishly in a manor house, with servants. There were small bunkhouses with dirt floors for the slaves, where many people were forced to inhabit a small space. Only the "privileged" slaves had private dwellings or lived in the big house with the plantation owner's family. Practically all of the field-work was done by slaves. It was usually at the hand of the overseer that slaves suffered their greatest abuse.

During the Civil War, as the great cotton and tobacco plantations burned, Southerners taught their children that this war was being fought because of Northern greed to dominate the prosperous South economically, and not to free the black slave from bondage or to maintain a united union. At the opulent, 1,700-acre former South Carolina Cotton Plantation, Boone Hall, it was written that "this was an unjust war being fought for a docile people who were simply content to have a hot meal, a fire and a warm place to sleep." Southerners believed that the slaves got "much positive enjoyment out of life." Their written sentiments were that "the slaves were extremely gregarious and delighted in plantation life. Slaves were permitted to have picnics on occasions and their love for singing, music, and dance contributed to the community." Misinformed Southerners thought that the life of a physically abused, overworked slave, sold into bondage from family and friends, offered more advantages for food, clothing, and shelter than the free, "savage" life that slaves left behind in Africa.

The typical Southerner arguing the merits of the Confederacy felt, and still feels, no deep compassion or empathy for the men and women whom they held captive and physically abused in slavery. Instead it was their tragic illusion of a glorious past life of "Southern gentility" to which their passions clung. They could not understand why Northerners, who had also previously owned slaves, cared about the well-being of a race of people the Southerners called "Darkies." This lack of understanding and utterly blatant disregard for the atrocious conditions of race relations for black people further widened the gap between the North and the South, ensuring the inevitability of the Civil War and the Civil Rights Movement to come. What the Southerner did not anticipate was the unrelenting need of the Negro to be freed from slavery and racial oppression. Black slaves eagerly assisted Northerners in liberating millions of slaves in the South, dismantling the racist regime of the Confederacy and in some cases leaving the Avenue of Oaks, the tree-lined drive to those once-opulent plantations, as the only memory left standing of these dreadful slave farms.

A nineteenth-century black woman; one of many whose beauty defied stereotypes.

The Negro came to the United States of America in 1619. Read any history book you want to read and you won't find it stated any better than that. We didn't come here on our own. But we were brought here from the jungles of Africa. We were happy, we were pleased, we were satisfied, and we were content in Africa.

But we were snatched from the bosom of our native soil, packed into ships and chained down against our will. Mr. Bennett says in his book that I am reading, *Before the Mayflower*, that hundreds of Negroes were thrown overboard and were caused to perish in the middle of the sea, simply because the mean and cruel task master, the white man, would walk down the aisle and stumble over Negroes chained to the ship and say, 'We have too many on board. Dump them over into the sea.'

We were brought here against our will, and when we got here we found no freedom.

And ever since sixteen hundred and nineteen, we have been misunderstood. We were forced to work in the fields from sunup to sundown. Who was it that cleared the new ground? There once was a time when where the city of Birmingham rests, there was nothing but a wilderness. Who was it that cut down the trees? Who was it that built the skyscrapers? Who was it that cut the streets and the avenues, cared for the sick, fed the hungry, and carried the garbage away? NOBODY BUT THE NEGRO. NOBODY BUT THE NEGRO. And he has remained faithful to this land. He fought in every war. Call them off. Name the wars he fought in.

Isaac and Rosa, two emancipated slave children.

"All the way from Boston Commons, when Crispus Attucks, a black man, was the first one to give his red blood in an effort to bring this nation into being.

"For it was on the sad Sunday morning at Pearl Harbor, the beach at Normandy, black boys and black fathers gave their red blood alongside their white brothers to preserve this nation.

"Ever since then, Negroes have been rising and falling, blundering and stumbling, mistreated, neglected, and dejected. But still saying, from the bottom of their hearts, 'God bless America, God bless America, my home sweet home.'

"Now this is our home. We want you to know that this is our home. We do not agree with those who want certain states. We don't want any particular state, as some advocate. We don't want any particular territory. We don't want to take over either. We just want to live as brothers. The Negroes of Birmingham are not going back to Africa. Our ancestors came from Africa. We didn't come from there. But until the Englishman goes back to England, until the Italian goes back to Italy, until the German goes back to Germany, the Mexican back to Mexico, the Frenchman goes back to France, the Spaniard goes back to Spain, and the white man gives back this country to the Indian, the black man will live in America."

—Ralph David Abernathy
Birmingham, 1963
16th Street Baptist Church

4

The first Negroes arrived one year prior to the Pilgrim fathers' landing at Plymouth Rock, Massachusetts. There existed a kindred spirit of respect between the Native American Indians and the black slaves, unlike the antagonistic interests of some white settlers to annihilate, dominate, and control the Native Americans and blacks in order to conquer North America. Millions upon millions of American Indians were brutally slaughtered for defending their country or infected with foreign diseases contracted from the settlers. With the remaining Indians relocated to reservations under illusive treaties, the white settlers staked their claim on the land.

For over 200 years Africans were imported to America for slave labor and the institution of slavery lasted for 244 years in the United States.

"Throughout slavery, the Negro was treated in a very inhumane fashion. He was considered a thing to be used, not a person to be respected. He was merely a depersonalized cog in a vast plantation machine. The famous Dred Scott decision of 1857 clearly expressed the status of the Negro during slavery. In this decision the United States Supreme Court affirmed that the Negro was not a citizen of the United States, he was merely property subject to the dictates of his owner."

—Martin Luther King Jr.
San Francisco, 1963

"I was born a slave. I am not sure of the exact date or place of my ancestry, I know almost nothing except my mother. In the slave quarters, I heard whispers of the tortures suffered in the middle passage of the slave ship from Africa to America. My mother was the plantation cook. All the cooking for the whites and slaves my mother had to do over an open fire. There was no wooden floor in our cabin, the naked earth being used as a floor. We slept in and on a bundle of filthy rags laid upon the dirt floor. From the time that I can remember anything, almost every day of my life has been occupied in some kind of labour."

"When war began between the North and the South, though other issues were discussed, the primal one was that of slavery. We kept ourselves informed of events by what was termed the 'grapevine' telegraph. I was awakened one night by my mother kneeling over her children, fervently praying that Lincoln and his armies might be successful, and that one day, she and her children might be free. I had no schooling whatsoever while I was a slave, though I had the feeling that to get into a schoolhouse and study would be about the same as getting into paradise."

—Booker T. Washington

Reconstruction

In 1867, two years after the end of the Civil War, Congress passed the Reconstruction Act, which compelled President Andrew Johnson to place officials in charge of the former states of the Confederacy. These officials were given the authority to govern and overrule the local existing governments in the South. They registered all people of the region to vote, entering the basic principles of democracy for the first time in the South.

New black voters voted their conscience and not that of their former owners, who wished to return them to servitude. Southeners said that blacks were controlled by Northern radi-

cals, but blacks didn't need coercion to vote against the former regime and elect blacks to public office. In the South Carolina Legislature, elected blacks outnumbered whites 88 to 67. The underprivileged classes finally had representation: there was relief for the poor, free public schools, and the rebuilding of public infrastructure destroyed by the war. These accomplishments were never appreciated by Southern white aristocracy.

Congress failed to anticipate the emergence of white vigilante groups, retaliating against the rising status of blacks, or their savage tactics. When Union troops departed the South, leaders of the old Confederacy regained control.

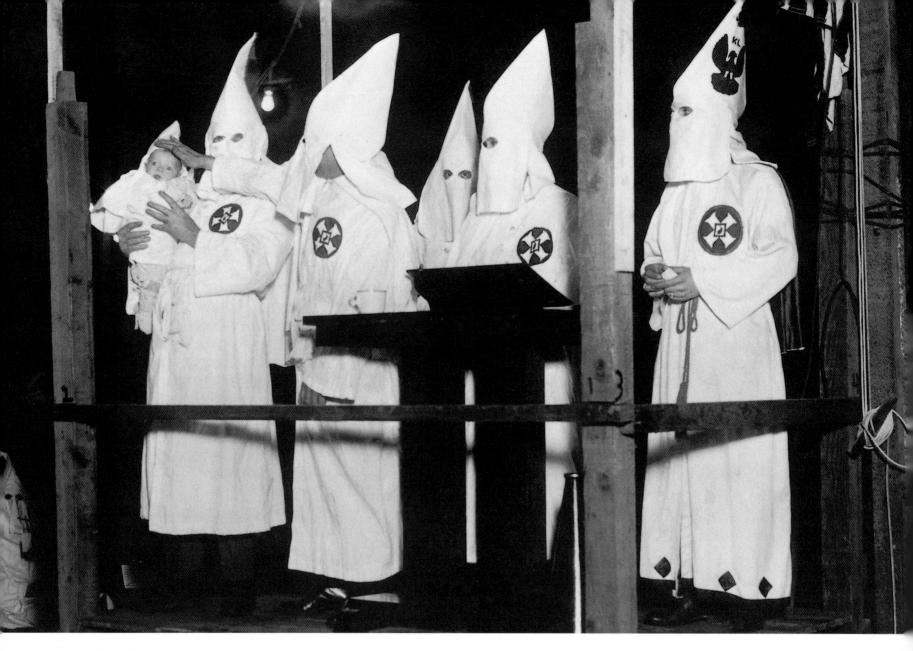

Post-Reconstruction

Despite the significant contributions of blacks to the American economy and labor force—creative architectural design of the nation's capital, inventions such as the filament in the lightbulb, the (steam heat) radiator, the traffic signal, blood plasma, the printing press, the elevator, the refrigerator, the electric railway system, and the rotary and two-cycle gas engines—they were continually assaulted by racist organizations such as the Ku Klux Klan, founded by the Confederate general Nathan Bedford Forrest.

The Oath of Secrecy of the KKK

"I most solemnly swear that I will forever keep sacredly secret the songs, words and grip . . . I will never yield to bribe, flattery, threats, passion, punishment, persecution, persuasion, nor any other enticement whatever coming from or offered by any person or persons, male or female, for the purpose of obtaining from me a secret or secret information. I will die rather than divulge them, so help me God."   —Oath taken from recorded testimony in the murder trial of Viola Gregg Liuzzo

The Scottsboro Boys

Scottsboro, Alabama, 1931. Nine Negro males were falsely accused of raping two white women, Victoria Price and Ruby Bates, on a freight train in Jackson County. Although there was no evidence against them, they were tried, convicted, and sentenced to death by an all-white jury. Through the efforts of the NAACP legal defense fund, the young men were saved from execution and eventually freed years later. (Above) The defendants in the Scottsboro case leave the Morgan County jail for the Decatur, Alabama, courthouse.

"When you have gotten the full story of the heroic conduct of the Negro . . . have heard it from the lips of Northerners and Southerners, from ex-Abolitionists and ex-Masters, then decide within yourself whether a race that is thus willing to die for its country should not be given the highest opportunity to live for its country."

—Booker T. Washington
October 16, 1897

Maybe in the near future we'll get back to the way things were in '37. At least I hope so.

Accused in 1937 of murdering a white in Mississippi, this black man was tortured with a blow-torch and then lynched.

This piece of hate mail sent to Ralph David Abernathy memorialized the era of vicious lynchings in the American south.

The Story of Emmett Till

A well-dressed, middle-class, frail boy from Chicago, stricken with polio at an early age, and with a stammering speech impediment, went on his summer vacation to visit relatives in the Mississippi Delta. Seven days after his arrival, Emmett Till rode 2.8 miles to the local store with his cousin and friends, where Emmett bought everyone bubble gum. When leaving the store, he said, "G-g-g-g...good-bye" to the white woman behind the counter. One of the local white boys said, "Bobo—don't you know? You're not supposed to say 'Good-bye' to a white woman?" Another white boy said, "But she was good-looking, wasn't she?" Emmett attempted to whistle in agreement.

Days later, Emmett Till's mutilated body was found floating feet up in the air in the Talla-hatchie River with his neck secured to a 90-pound cotton gin fan wrapped in barbed wire. Emmett Till was 14 years old. It was believed that he was pistol-whipped and shot in the head by the woman's husband, Roy Bryant, and J. W. Milam, both of whom were subsequently exonerated of the charges.

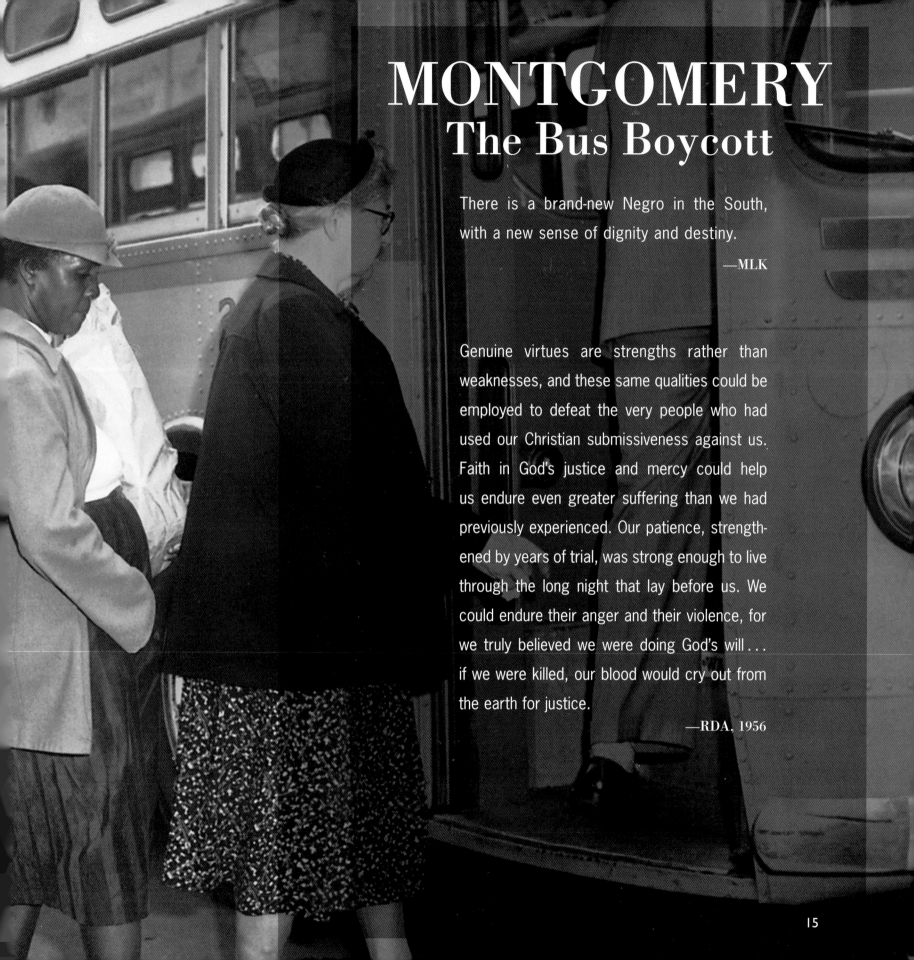

MONTGOMERY
The Bus Boycott

There is a brand-new Negro in the South, with a new sense of dignity and destiny.

—MLK

Genuine virtues are strengths rather than weaknesses, and these same qualities could be employed to defeat the very people who had used our Christian submissiveness against us. Faith in God's justice and mercy could help us endure even greater suffering than we had previously experienced. Our patience, strengthened by years of trial, was strong enough to live through the long night that lay before us. We could endure their anger and their violence, for we truly believed we were doing God's will... if we were killed, our blood would cry out from the earth for justice.

—RDA, 1956

Montgomery, a traditional Southern city, had once been the official headquarters of the Confederacy. With the blatant abuse of Negroes, social unrest was growing in the community. The issues developed into a serious impasse through the deepening of fears, and the insistence by Negroes on the improvement of their status and welfare. Negroes in Montgomery became increasingly sensitive and resentful toward acts of discrimination and segregation. The Supreme Court decision of 1954 declaring segregation in the public schools unconstitutional deepened the dissatisfaction of both whites and Negroes over the state of affairs.

My father's mentor, Vernon Johns, an eloquent preacher and advocate for social action, was absolutely fearless in the face of racism. When he abruptly resigned from the pastorate of Dexter Avenue Baptist Church, the church called Martin Luther King Jr. for a trial sermon. Dr. Johns, meanwhile, asked my father for permission to speak at First Baptist on the morning of Martin's trial sermon, unbeknownst to Ralph. From his new home in Virginia, Dr. Johns called Rev. M. L. King Sr. and asked if he could ride to Montgomery with Martin. I don't know what they discussed along that journey but if it was like the many conversations between Dr. Johns and my father, it would have been about the crisis of the Negro, and what needed to be done.

My father wrote that they were waiting in Montgomery and wondering how Vernon would arrive. Mother was in the kitchen, preparing Vernon's favorite meal. Knowing Vernon's habit of hitchhiking, they expected to hear the telephone ring and Vernon asking for Daddy to pick him up. It was almost four in the afternoon when they heard a car pull into the driveway. Ralph said, "Through the blinds I saw Vernon get out of the front seat carrying a suitcase and then the driver got out as well. The driver, a short lean young man, looked familiar. I tried to figure out why. Then I realized that I had met him before. He was Martin Luther King Jr. I met them at the door, shook hands, and invited them in.

"I'm going to spend the night with one of the Dexter Avenue deacons," Martin said, "but I could stop in for just a minute." Mother came out of the kitchen to greet them and threw her arms around Vernon. The aroma of chopped sirloin steak permeated the air. "That certainly does smell good," said Vernon. Martin agreed.

Juanita said, "We have more than enough, and you are welcome to stay."

Martin said that he would like to, but that he had a previous engagement. At that moment, Juanita returned to the kitchen, brought out the food, and announced, "Dinner's served, and Rev. King, I've already set a place for you." Martin laughed, threw up his hands, and joined them for dinner.

Afterward, the talk became more serious. Ralph said that they talked about the oppression of the people and about the growing belief that change was taking place. They agreed that *Brown v. the Board of Education* had forever changed the conditions on which the struggle could be fought. The federal government might finally render service in the fight for freedom.

In his autobiography, Ralph wrote, "Vernon and I had talked about these matters before, but Martin, a relative stranger, was forthcoming in his advocacy of an active program to force the issue and bring about freedom more rapidly. He was committed to the preaching of a social Gospel that would awaken the Christian churches and mobilize them in the fight against segregation. He said he had been working on plans to do just that and when time came to do battle, he hoped the churches would be ready. We talked about action, though only in the vaguest of terms. Martin stayed as long as he could, then reluctantly rose, thanked Juanita for the marvelous meal, and drove off. The next morning at the white radio station, I preached a short sermon for the people who got up at 7:00 A.M. or those that didn't want to go to church. At the end of my sermon I had a telephone call. It was Martin who told me how much he had enjoyed dinner last night and my sermon this morning. He was thoughtful. I hoped that he would be called to Dexter Avenue Baptist Church. Many of the members of Dexter Avenue came over to First Baptist that Sunday to hear Vernon, a man who they loved. But those who did missed one of the greatest sermons. Martin was at his best, and at his best, no one was more eloquent. His topic was 'The Three Dimensions of a Complete Life,' and when he was finished, the congregation was in awe of him. Martin got the call, and the Lord had sent me a friend. I offered up a prayer of gratitude. Like Vernon, Martin was someone I could not only talk to but learn from. He was finishing his doctorate at Boston University, and we shared the same hopes for the future, and the vision of a transformed society. I eagerly awaited his arrival in Montgomery. I had the same feeling about his move to Montgomery that I had on that Sunday when I first met him in Atlanta. We were meant to be friends, partners in some extraordinary enterprise."

From the beginning they were inseparable. Though both of them had heavy responsibilities as pastors they tried to meet every day. Because of Jim Crow they could only have dinner at home. So the four of them had dinner every night, with Juanita preparing the meal one evening, Coretta the next. Usually their conversations would last way beyond midnight.

It was an exciting time, because we were talking about important projects, spelling them out in terms of actions we could take in Montgomery. Martin had ideas about the means of attaining freedom, while I had an understanding of Montgomery. Together we formulated a plan to turn the city into a model of social justice and racial amity. We recognized the seeming impossibility of the task, but also understood that change was inevitable, imminent and that we could provide the proper means of achieving these social ends without destroying the community.

"We insisted implementation be completely nonviolent. Martin and I thoroughly read and absorbed the teachings of Henry David Thoreau and Mahatma Gandhi on this subject. We had seen the possibilities in applying the same ideas and practices to the elimination of segregation in America. We thoroughly explored all the ramifications and pitfalls, and knew what had to be done.

As Martin expounded philosophy, I spoke of practical application. While he was talking about strategy, the broad overall campaign, I was envisioning tactics and how to achieve the strategy through specific actions. Coretta and Juanita also contributed significantly to these plans, which were the product of detailed dialogue. When we spoke of implementing the plans, we were thinking in terms of years rather than weeks or even months.

"Martin believed that he had to establish credibility in the black community before he could lead a nonviolent crusade for freedom. He wanted the respect and trust of progressive white leaders who might prove invaluable in the struggle. As a former teacher at Alabama State College, I wanted more academic credentials, so I began planning for my doctorate while taking a leave of absence from First Baptist.

Two unidentified men, RDA, and Vernon Johns.

t all seemed so reasonable and yet so remote on those autumn nights when we sat together and outlined the future. Then, as we put the final touches on our plans, God intervened with a plan of his own and a more urgent timetable. People believe that the Civil Rights Movement came about by sheer accident, from events in the 1950s. Certainly chance played a role in the timing of the Movement, but the shape it took was partly the result of our conversations during the weeks before we suddenly found our-selves at the center of the Rosa Parks controversy.

Negroes in 1955 faced what they felt to be a common problem: the deplorable conditions on city buses. The Women's Political Council, a group of middle-class Negro women in Montgomery, began efforts to clarify the seating policy on buses. Montgomery, unlike Birmingham and some of the other cities, did not have the big glaring signs that divided Negroes and whites into various sec-tions of the bus. The bus drivers had the authority to determine where imaginary lines of racial division would be.

During the month of March, 1955, a 14-year-old Negro schoolgirl, Miss Claudette Colvin, was dragged from a bus, handcuffed, arrested, and thrown into jail. Miss Colvin occu-pied a seat in what was commonly used as the Negro section. When the bus driver demanded that she give up her seat to a white man, she refused. We held several conferences following her arrest with the city and the officials of the bus company. We asked that they do two things: change the seating policy to a first-come, first-served basis; that is, with Negroes

beginning from the rear and whites from the front with no reserved seats for either group. Wherever the two races met, this would constitute the dividing line. Then we asked that they clarify the seating policy and publish it in the paper so that each person would know where his section was. After several conferences, bus officials refused. The white drivers were determined to harass people at every opportunity. They would make blacks pay their fare, get off, and go to the back door to enter. Sometimes they would even take off as a passenger walked outside the bus to the rear door after paying. Once a driver closed the back door on a black woman's arm and dragged her to the next stop before allowing her to climb aboard. Clearly this kind of cru-elty was contributing to increasing tension on Montgomery buses. We tried to reason with local authorities. They were polite, listened to our complaints, and did nothing.

"On December 1, 1955, Mrs. Rosa Parks set events in motion that would lead to a social revolution of monumental proportions. Thursday evening, with her shoulder aching and a long day behind her, she found a seat on the only row that wasn't filled—the 11th row from the front. This is significant because of the peculiarity of Mont-gomery's Jim Crow law pertaining to buses. In Montgomery, the first 10 rows were reserved for whites only whether or not there were any white riders on the bus. So Mrs. Parks was acting within the law when she sat down in an outside seat in the 11th row, with a black man to her right (next to the window) and two black women across the aisle.

at the third stop, the Empire Theater, a white man got off, and the driver glanced back and saw that whites occupied rows one through 10 of the already crowded bus. Looking at the passengers in row 11, he called out, 'All right you n____s, I want those seats.'

No one replied or moved....What the driver was commanding was neither legal nor logical. 'Y'all better make it light on yourselves and let me have those seats,' the driver said.

After a second's hesitation the two women and the man rose, but Mrs. Parks remained seated. Then she slid over next to the window. The move spoke for itself. 'Look, woman, I want the seat. Are you going to stand up?' 'No,' she said quietly. He exploded. 'If you don't stand up I'm going to have you arrested.' Soon a patrol car drove up and two officers got out. After talking to the driver, he pointed out Mrs. Parks. The policemen came down the aisle and asked her, 'Why didn't you stand up?' 'Why do you push us around?' she asked him. 'I don't know,' he said, 'but the law is the law, and you are under arrest.' Mrs. Parks rose quietly and was taken to

jail. It is important to understand the kind of person Mrs. Parks was in order to understand fully why her arrest caused so much reaction in the black community. As a 42-year-old seamstress at a large department store, she was a slight woman, soft-spoken and courteous. Though she was the secretary of the local NAACP chapter, she was not the kind of bold and aggressive activist who usually challenged civil authority. She had an air of gentility about her that usually evoked respect. I doubt that anyone who knew her could have imagined that she would ever end up in jail.

On Friday, December 2, before I got out of bed, I received a telephone call about five o'clock in the morning from Mr.

E. D. Nixon, a Pullman porter and the president of the local chapter of the National Association for the Advancement of Colored People. Mr. Nixon informed me of Mrs. Parks' arrest. Nixon said he had signed for her bond, so she had not spent the night in jail. Clifford Durr, a white lawyer friendly to blacks, had advised them that she clearly couldn't be charged under local law since no other seat had been available to her. But even though Montgomery statutes were on her side, state law gave a bus driver arbitrary powers over passengers. So she was subject to prosecution for disobeying his command, even though he had been wrong in ordering her to move. Nixon said he was ready to take action. He told me that he thought that we should do something because we had taken enough. 'Now is the time to stay off of the buses,' he said 'and show the white people that we will not tolerate the way we had been treated any longer.' I agreed with him.

"Jo Ann Robinson, a professor of English at Alabama State University, who headed the Women's Political Council, met with Mrs. Parks after her release the previous night, and was preparing a leaflet calling for specific action in response to the incident. In part it read:

This woman's case will come up Monday. We are, therefore, asking every Negro to stay off the buses Monday in protest of the arrest and trial. Don't ride the buses to work, to town, to school, or anywhere on Monday. You can afford to stay out of school for one day if you have no other way to go except by bus. You can also afford to stay out of town for one day. If you work, take a cab, or share a ride, or walk. But please, children and grown-ups, don't ride the bus at all on Monday.

"Nixon was scheduled for a trip that would keep him on the road for the next three days, so he wanted me to take charge. How should we proceed in order to rally public support? Whom should we call?' I thought for a moment. 'I believe we should ask Dr. Hubbard to call a meeting of black leaders under the auspices of the Baptist Ministers Conference.' 'Anybody else you can think of besides Hubbard?' Nixon asked. 'Why don't you ask Martin Luther King?' I said. 'I don't know Reverend King, but since I'll be out of town, I'm going to leave the situation in your hands. Do what you think is best. We have to get our people to stop riding those buses for at least a day or two. That's the only way we'll ever get what we want.' I agreed and said I would get to work on it. As soon as he hung up, I called Martin and told him the story of Mrs. Parks. 'We have to do something this time,' I said. 'In which case,' he said, 'let my contribution be the meeting place.' Next I called Dr. Hubbard and E. D. Nixon called Martin. I telephoned all the black Baptist preachers and told them there would be a very important meeting that night at Dexter Avenue Church. I made no mention of why we were gathering because I didn't want the white establishment to find out in advance and try to intimidate us, either individually or collectively.

The AME Zionists were gathering that morning at Hilliard Chapel AME Zion Church to meet with their bishop. When I arrived, I found Jo Ann Robinson outside, passing out leaflets announcing our meeting. The message had spread all over the black community by word of mouth, so effective was the grapevine.

Inside the chapel I gave what came to be known as the first speech calling for the Civil Rights Movement. When I came out of the church, Mrs. Robinson was waiting for me. She told me she was planning to give out boycott leaflets to the children leaving school, and I offered to help. As a fellow college teacher, I knew she was extremely vulnerable; so we kept her authorship of the leaflet a secret, and gave a leaflet to every child in sight. After dinner, I went by to pick up Martin. The Brethren [ministers] turned out in large numbers waiting for the action to begin. We divided the city into various districts and assigned individuals to pass out handbills in the various Negro sections in order that people might be persuaded not to ride the buses on Monday, but to come to the mass meeting on Holt Street on Monday night. One Negro woman got a handbill and turned it over to the white woman for whom she worked. The white woman turned it over to the city authorities, and they gave it to the *Montgomery Advertiser.* The newspaper printed the handbill on the front page of the Sunday morning paper, thus we got free front-page coverage. One elderly Negro woman said she hadn't gotten a handbill but upon seeing the notice printed verbatim in the paper, she knew that she was not supposed to ride the buses. "Sunday evening, the Police Commissioner appeared on local television and radio stations to assure Negro people that he would 'give them police protection if they rode the buses on Monday.' It had been reported to him, he claimed, that there were 'Negro goon squads' organized to keep Negroes from riding the buses, and he was assuring people that it was all right to ride. We had gotten excellent newspaper, radio, and even television coverage. The Commissioner also said that there would be two squad cars, one in front and one behind every bus that Monday morning. This worked in our favor; Negroes who had not really been swept into the spirit of the Movement, upon seeing policemen riding behind the buses, felt they were there to force them to ride, and rebelled against it by joining those who were walking.

Rosa Parks with Ed Nixon.

Thus, by Sunday evening we were reasonably certain we had spread the word throughout the entire black community. The only question that remained was how well our people would respond. No one knew the answer and several of us slept uneasily that night.

On Monday morning we awoke wondering what the day would bring. About an hour before sunrise, Martin came by my house and we watched out the window as the Jackson Street bus made its first run from Alabama State. When we peered over at the stop, no one was there. Not a single passenger. We held our breath as we watched the road and then the headlights rose around the corner. The driver slowed down, then picked up speed and roared on past. There were no passengers on the bus. We looked at each other and grinned. The boycott was working. It was working perfectly. For the first time in the history of Montgomery, blacks were working together to resist racial injustice.

Juanita broke the silence with a loud 'Thank you, Jesus!' It was indeed a new day. But only the beginning.

Shortly before nine, we went to the city courthouse, as it was the morning of Mrs. Parks' trial. We could not get in as there were too many people.

RDA, MLK, and Bayard Rustin.

Policemen demanded that people get off the street and not block the sidewalks. The city officials were overly disgruntled. Court convened at 9:00, and by 9:05 it was over. Local officials had huddled with lawyers for the state, Mrs. Parks had been charged with refusing to obey a bus driver, a state offense, rather than with a violation of local seating regulations. The judge listened to the brief recitation of the facts and pronounced Mrs. Parks guilty. He'd assessed a fine of 10 dollars plus court costs, hoping to move on quickly. However, her attorney, Fred Gray, announced that he would appeal the ruling on the grounds that Jim Crow laws were unconstitutional, then the trial ended. Short and perfunctory, it was one of the most significant court cases in American history, given its long-range consequences.

"With the success of our boycott, we were certain we could make a difference. All we needed was the right kind of organization. As we left the courthouse, I heard more than one person ask, 'What are we going to do next?'

"Martin and I had already come up with some possible answers to that question between stops on Saturday night. On Sunday evening, Juanita and I had organized a plan on paper: officers, meetings, committees, activities. We had everything outlined, and it was a good plan.

"I told Nixon that Martin and I believed that the first order of business should be the establishment of a new organization, one that would not be associated with the issues or the failures of the past. Nixon was naturally reluctant, since the NAACP was our oldest and most respected national organization. But in Montgomery it had recorded few accomplishments. In fact, we had made more progress that morning than the Montgomery NAACP had made in its history. I said we should demand:

"1. A pledge from the city authorities and from bus company officials that blacks would be treated with courtesy when we rode the bus. No more name-calling. No more closing the door in our faces.

"2. A new ordinance that would allow blacks to be seated from the rear forward, and whites from the front rearward. No reserved areas. Nobody standing when there were empty places on the bus.

3. Since many routes (e.g., Jackson Street) were almost exclusively for black passengers, blacks should be allowed to apply for positions as bus drivers.

"Knowing how they would react gave us the opportunity to engage in a strategy. We knew that our first two demands were reasonable, so reasonable that the Establishment might well be willing to grant them—except they could not appear to be giving in to black pressure. It was a matter of their racial pride, their manhood. So we had to provide them with a way to give us what we wanted, while being tough and unyielding. We did this by adding one additional demand at the end of two very reasonable ones. They would give us what we wanted and still save face by denying us something we never thought we could get in the first place.

"I went home to lunch, then picked up Martin. We arrived at the meeting immediately after Reverend Bennett had given the devotion. At that time the president of the National Association for the Advancement of Colored People sounded an alarm. He exclaimed, 'We have some stool pigeons [subversives] in the house. They are here to get our strategy to take it back to the white man. Don't go any further.' A motion prevailed that we elect an executive committee that would go into a secret session in the pastor's study and work out a program for the mass meeting. We gave it authority without having to report to the larger group for approval. The eighteen person selected committee retired to the pastor's study where I told the assembled group about the need for a new organization to represent the black community during the current crisis. I said we had talked among ourselves for the past several days and had come up with a structure and a plan of action for the immediate future. I reminded them of

the success of the Monday boycott and pointed out that because we had been able to act together, we were on the verge of an important victory. For that reason, I said, 'we need an organization that would unify our people, and that meant business.'

"Bennett moved that we adopt my plan as presented, and it passed without a dissenting vote.

"The next item that came before the committee was the name. Several names were submitted. Then I gave the name, 'The Montgomery Improvement Association,' so that it would reflect the name of the city. I wanted an organization that would be concerned with the total social, economic, spiritual, and political improvement of all the people of Montgomery.

"The name Montgomery Improvement Association was adopted. Thus on this day, December 5, 1955, the social movement took an organizational form. The next question before the committee was the election of a president. The house was open to receive nominations. Mr. Rufus Lewis arose and said, 'Mr. Chairman, I wish to move that my pastor, Reverend Martin Luther King Jr., be chosen as president of this organization.' Martin was caught off guard. Neither he nor I expected this.

"He hesitated for a moment, then answered quietly. 'Well, if you think I can render some service, I will.' He smiled and shrugged his shoulders. He had no prior knowledge of Lewis's intentions. The vote was unanimous. Martin presided.

"As it turned out, this [organizational] structure meant that Martin and I did most of the work, he as the chief officer, I

is the chief organizer of activities. With a good organization in place and with Martin to head it, everyone felt a
sudden surge of joy. Something important had happened in
that room and we sensed it. We had come upstairs, con-
fused and shaken by the idea that there was a traitor in our
midst. We came down with a sense of dedication and unity.
We had been together in the Upper Room and we were
going into the world to do the Lord's work.

That evening I had been working up until the last minute on
the resolutions. We had had a successful 'one-day protest,'
but we feared that if we extended it beyond the first day,
we might fail. We were to determine whether to continue
the protest by the size of the crowds. . . . When we got
about 20 blocks from the church we saw cars parked solid and we wondered if there was a funeral or a death in the community. But, as we got closer to the church we saw a great mass of people. The Montgomery Advertiser estimated the crowd at approximately seven thousand persons all trying to get into a church that will accommodate less than a thousand. It took us about 15 minutes to work our way through the crowd: Please let us through. We are Reverend King and Reverend Abernathy. Please permit us to get through.' Once through the crowd there was
another 10 minutes of picture-taking coupled with flashing lights, cheering, and hand-clapping. Those inside
applauded for at least 10 minutes.

It was apparent to us that the people were with us. It was
then that all of the ministers who had previously refused
to take part in the program for fear of retaliation due to

exposure in the newspapers, came up to Reverend King
and me to offer their services. This expression of togeth-
erness on the part of the masses was obviously an inspiration. Mrs. Rosa Parks was presented to the mass
meeting because we wanted her to become symbolic
of our protest movement. Following her, we presented
Mr. Daniels, who at 19 years of age had been arrested
earlier that day. The policeman alleged that he tried to
prevent a Negro woman from riding the bus, while he
a college student, was only assisting her across the
street. The appearance of these persons added momentum
to the Movement.

"We then heard the resolutions calling for the continuation of the boycott. The
resolution stated, 'Negro
people and people of good
conscience are to refrain
from riding the buses until
grievances were granted
(1) more courtesy on the
part of the bus drivers
(2) first-come, first-served
seating policy; and (3) the
employment of Negro bus
drivers on predominantly
Negro bus routes.'

"These three resolutions
were unanimously and en-
thusiastically adopted by the
seven thousand people crammed inside and outside the
church.

"We closed the meeting by taking an offering, with people
marching down the aisles giving their nickels, dimes,
quarters, and dollars for freedom."

—RD4

"There comes a time when people get tired of being trampled over by the iron feet of oppression. There comes a time when people get tired of being pushed out of the glittering sunlight of life's July and left standing in the piercing chills of an Alpine November. . . . Work and fight until justice runs down like water, and righteousness like a mighty stream."

—MLK

The First Mass Meeting

"Our method is one of passive resistance, of nonviolence, not economic reprisals. Let us keep love in our hearts but fight until the walls of segregation crumble."

—RDA
First Baptist Church

Following pages: A mass meeting at First Baptist Church RDA, Pastor

On January 9, a white Montgomery attorney alerted the court and media to an old state law against boycotts. It was based on Title 14, Section 54, which read, "When two or more persons enter into a conspiracy to prevent the operation of a lawful business, without just cause or legal excuse, they shall be guilty of a misdemeanor." The grand jury of Montgomery County determined that the boycott was illegal and indicted more than a hundred persons during the week of February 13. On February 22, the police began to round up the leaders involved with the Montgomery Improvement Association (MIA). In his book *Stride Toward Freedom,* Martin stated, "As usual, Ralph was unperturbed." My father remembered being quite humble when the policeman arrived at the door to arrest him for the first time. When he went to his bedroom to gather his things, he knelt and prayed for forgiveness from his deceased parents for any disgrace that he might cause his family. Burdened by great anxiety, Martin and his father met with top NAACP legal council before driving back to Montgomery to be arrested. Upon their arrival, they were greeted by Ralph, who had just been released (below). Martin asked Ralph to drive back to the courthouse and stand with him for his arrest (left). Ralph told an apprehensive Martin how people had rushed to get arrested the day before, and had voluntarily gone to the sheriff's office to see if their names were on the list. A once fear-ridden people had been transformed.

"Social unrest had reached a critical level. Leaders were no longer afraid, no longer fearful of their pictures in the papers because we knew we were not standing alone. We now felt that we had the whole community behind us. The people had rallied to make us their leaders and had given the leaders the courage to stand up in the face of what appeared to be insurmountable opposition. It was under these conditions that the restless dissatisfaction and frustration of a segregated people became socialized and collectivized in a state of popular excitement."

—RDA

Negroes walked and walked...

The New Republic reported on February 24, 1956, that "the ghost of Gandhi walks" the streets of Montgomery. Their symbol was Mahatma Gandhi, the wise man in the loincloth from India. As disciples of Mahatma, they would employ non-violent resistance, a simple refusal to cooperate with the evils of segregation.

The first problem to solve was how the former bus riders would get around the city. As the taxis were segregated, they called on Negro taxis for low-rate jitney service, until the police threatened that a minimum of 45 cents must be charged. So they organized, with "military precision," a carpool of over three hundred private cars that would pick up and transport passengers from early morning into the late evening. They also purchased station wagons in the names of the churches. This helped to increase the efficiency of the carpool, as the station wagons ran on a full-time basis, employing people who had previously been unemployed. When the local insurance companies discovered that the new station wagons were being used by the Montgomery Improvement Association in the boycott, their insurance was canceled. After several rejections, they were awarded the necessary liability insurance by Lloyds of London, the oldest insurance company in the world, via the Alexander Company. They spent more than $5,000 a week on gasoline, dispatch, salaries, and auto repairs to operate the boycott. However, the segregated bus company's finances fell into dire straits from the lack of Negro patronage. They had to cancel half of their routes, lay off drivers, and raise the fares on the routes that white passengers took. The buses were given the name "yellow ghost" by local whites, and they lost an average of $3,500 per day for 381 days. The estimated total loss in revenue was $1,333,500.

Without the dollars of Negroes, the Montgomery economy began to collapse. Therefore, fear permeated the consciousness of the white merchants. Segregationists claim that there was no segregation in the stores—even the best ones—because they knew and openly admitted that they would suffer severe financial losses without Negro patronage. In the department stores, they bragged that blacks and whites stood together in checkout lines and crowded elevators without a second thought because elevators were not segregated. There was, however, segregation at the drinking fountains and in rest rooms and dressing rooms. There was no segregation in the banks or at the teller windows. The Montgomery economy depended on having the wealthy Negro patrons in their banks. That same bank, however, would refuse to give Negroes jobs, and made borrowing money extremely difficult. That is why it was important to establish black banks, and for Negroes to patronize black businesses. Montgomery's Mayor Gayle appointed a committee to meet with Martin, Ralph, and the Montgomery Improvement Association. However, the committee consisted of white Citizens' Council members, a white-collar version of the blue-collar Ku Klux Klan, of which the mayor was a member. A reporter wrote that all of the Citizens' Council members had taken a pledge "to fight for segregation to the bitter end." And it was for them a bitter end, because they refused to accept the inevitable and listen to the Montgomery Improvement Association's minimal demands. They felt that there was no need for any negotiations with Negroes and the talks were broken off. So the Negro continued to protest, walking throughout spring and summer.

Martin was deeply concerned that no one exploit the Movement for their own gain. He said, "We need money, but we're not going to do anything and everything to get it. No one is going to get fat on this, and no one is going to get any hand-outs." Martin and Ralph never received a salary for all their years of work. They never became rich men, but they were able to succeed because they were chasing not fame and fortune, but a moral means of attaining their God-given rights as human beings. Their victory was not just for the Negro alone, it was also a victory for democracy.

Ralph and Martin emerge victorious from the courthouse.

On Tuesday, November 13, 1956, the U.S. Supreme Court affirmed the decision of a special, three-judge U.S. District Court that declared Alabama's state and local laws allowing segregation on buses unconstitutional. By December 20, the court order reached Montgomery and on the morning of December 23, blacks took the first ride. Workshops were held in every black pulpit on the Sunday before the ride. Anticipating violence, the newspapers published the MIA's Rules of Nonviolent Conduct. Martin wrote, "I asked Ralph Abernathy, E. D. Nixon, and Glenn Smiley to join me in riding on the first integrated bus. They reached my house around 5:45 on Friday morning. At 5:55, we walked toward the bus stop." Martin, Ralph, Nixon, and Smiley boarded the bus with several reporters and television cameras in tow. Ralph rode with Mrs. Bascom, and Martin rode with Glenn. This first ride brought a symbolic end to the 381-day protest. (Above, seated in the First Baptist, Gilen and Helen Smiley with Juanita, baby Juandalynn, and Ralph.)

"Shortly after the beginning of the Montgomery Bus Boycott, Martin's friend, Bayard Rustin, brought in Glenn E. Smiley [above left] from the Fellowship of Reconciliation to teach them the principles of nonviolence. As a pacifist and a follower of Gandhi, Glenn had firsthand knowledge of Gandhi's philosophies and nonviolent civil disobedience. It wasn't enough for people to know merely how they should behave, but why. Knowing something and having the strength to put it into practice are two entirely different matters. We decided to hold workshops in nonviolent protest to make certain that people were prepared for any indignity the white community might have in store for us, including physical violence. We instituted "dress rehearsals" knowing that when people are smote on one cheek the natural tendency is not to turn the other cheek but to smite back. We drilled people so thoroughly in the philosophy and techniques of nonviolence that when they were attacked, their instinctive reaction would be to protect themselves as effectively as possible without lashing out at the enemy. Workshops were held on Saturdays. Martin and I were usually the instructors, though we invited Glenn to join us. We planned this training very carefully, utilizing the chief virtues of our people, which were a deep, abiding faith, and an almost infinite supply of patience. We talked to our people a great deal about the power of redemptive suffering. Our faith in the promise of Heaven had made us less concerned about our lot in this imperfect world because patient suffering was commended in the Bible."

—RDA

On the day of the first ride, there were three reported violent assaults against whites. What scared "die-hard whites" in Montgomery and elsewhere was that Negroes were publicly demanding their rights and that the previously disunited Negro population was sticking together in its demands despite great personal sacrifice. Enlightened, educated whites agreed that the practices of Jim Crow needed to be abolished; however, they knew and feared the violent reactions and hatred that would stem from "die-hard whites" if change was to come. The reassurance of nonviolent, passive resistance from Negroes was not their primary worry; rather, it was the violent resistance from bitter whites and the Ku Klux Klan.

In the predawn hours of January 10, 1957, my parents' home was severely damaged by a bomb. Ralph and Martin had gone to Atlanta to prepare for the first meeting of the Southern Christian Leadership Conference (SCLC). Alone in the house, with the baby sleeping in her crib, Juanita turned off the Jack Paar show and went to her bedroom. She said that about 15 minutes later "the living room exploded." She telephoned Ralph, who was staying with Martin at his father's (Granddaddy King's) house. Martin said, "In the middle of the night we were awakened by a telephone call from Juanita. I knew that only some new disaster would make her rouse us at two in the morning." Juanita told Ralph that the house had been bombed, and that three or four other explosions had been heard around the community. She reassured him that she was okay, as a neighbor was with them. But he insisted on flying back on the next plane. When Martin saw Ralph, his sober expression told him the story. "Thank God Juanita and Juandalynn are safe," he said. After making reservations, Ralph called back to Montgomery. As they were speaking, Mother heard another loud explosion. She asked, "What was that?" A policeman later told us it was First Baptist Church. When he found out Martin started to pack his bags, too, leaving the first meeting of the SCLC to be conducted by Coretta. Martin wrote, "With both his home and church bombed in one night, I knew no words to comfort him. There in the early morning hours we prayed to God together, asking for the power of endurance, the strength to carry on." The bomb was placed under the porch, inches from the gas line. Besides my parents' home, the home of Rev. Robert Graetz (a white minister of a Negro congregation) and three other churches—Bell Street, Hutchinson Street, Mt. Olive—were bombed. No amount of terror could stop the Civil Rights Movement.

The launching of this campaign in Montgomery was the warning sign of the turbulent years to come, and the birth of truth, justice, and equality for Negroes in the United States of America.

In June 1958, there was a prayer pilgrimage to Washington, D.C. Selected representatives of the pilgrimage met with President Eisenhower to discuss the court-ordered suspension of school integration at Little Rock. They appealed to Eisenhower to uphold the Supreme Court–ordered integration of the schools. Their plea fell on deaf ears, forcing them to take matters into their own hands. Above, left to right: Lester Granger, executive secretary of the National Urban League; Martin Luther King Jr.; E. Frederic Morrow, White House staff; President Eisenhower; A. Philip Randolph, founder of the Brotherhood of Sleeping Car Porters; William Rogers, attorney general; and Roy Wilkins, executive secretary of the National Association for the Advancement of Colored People.

"If you will protest courageously and yet with dignity and Christian love when the history books are written in future generations, the historians will have to pause and say: 'There lived a great people—a black people—who injected new meaning and dignity in the veins of civilization.'"

"Ultimately, the most prejudiced mind in Montgomery, the most prejudiced mind in America, will become a loving mind. And 24 years from now, men will look back and laugh . . . even at segregation!"

—MLK, Montgomery, 1955

Little Rock, Arkansas

Determined to make their contribution to justice, six of the Little Rock Nine sat on the wall of the U.S. Supreme Court, where Thurgood Marshall was filing an appeal to override an order by the St. Louis Circuit Court of Appeals that would delay the desegregation of Central High School. Left to right: Carlotta Walls, Melba Patillo, Jefferson Thomas, Minnijean Brown, Gloria Ray, and Elizabeth Eckford. (Missing: Ernest Green, Thelma Mothershed, Terrence Roberts, and their adviser, Mrs. Daisy Bates.)

(Opposite) On September 2, 1957, Arkansas governor Orval Faubus went against the U.S. Supreme Court order that allowed for the integration of public schools. He ordered the Arkansas National Guard to keep Negro students from integrating Little Rock's all-white Central High School. Because of the tense stand-off, on September 22, President Eisenhower was forced to send in the U.S. Army to escort Negro students to school. Despite the presence of the troops, the Little Rock Nine could not be protected from the racial slurs, violent threats, hateful pranks, and evil words they were forced to endure by their white classmates. Because of their courage, millions of black and white students would later be educated together all over America.

Terrence Roberts (left) reads a newspaper story about his attempt to enter high school.

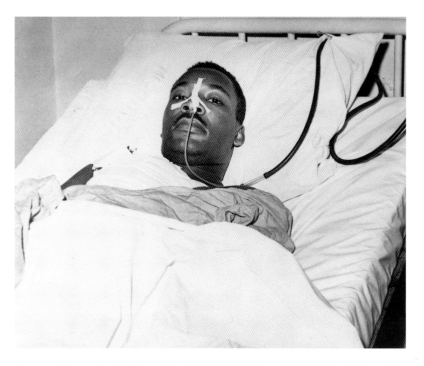

At the end of the bus boycott, Martin wrote his first book, *Stride Toward Freedom*. While he was in New York City for a book signing, a deranged black woman came up to Martin and stabbed him in the chest with a letter opener. He was hospitalized in New York's Harlem Hospital (left). Years later when he told us about the stabbing, he said that the doctors feared he would have died if he had sneezed.

(Opposite) October 24, 1958. Martin returned home to Montgomery from the hospital to friends and well-wishers. Ralph carried Martin Luther King III as Martin walked with the Rev. S. S. Seay, executive secretary of the MIA.

There was an evangelical quality to the bus boycott and the whites recognized it as ominous. The heart and soul of black people carried this movement. Montgomery was the first citywide passive-resistance campaign against the Jim Crow laws of segregation.

Nothing better illustrated the new temperament of the blacks of the Deep South than the boycott by 42,000 Negroes of the Montgomery Bus Lines. It was executed with almost-perfect success over 381 days. What started as a simple day-to-day mission evolved into the largest movement for human and civil rights in the history of the United States of America. The soul of the Negro was on fire in Montgomery, Alabama.

"Wherever segregation exists, we must be willing to rise up in mass and protest courageously against it. I realize that this type of courage means suffering and sacrifice. It might mean going to jail. If such is the case we must honorably fill up the jail houses of the South. It might even lead to physical death. But if such physical death is the price that we must pay to free our children from a life of permanent psychological death, then nothing could be more honorable. This is really the meaning of the method of passive resistance. It confronts physical force with an even stronger force, namely, soul force."

—MLK

Stride Toward Freedom: The Montgomery Story

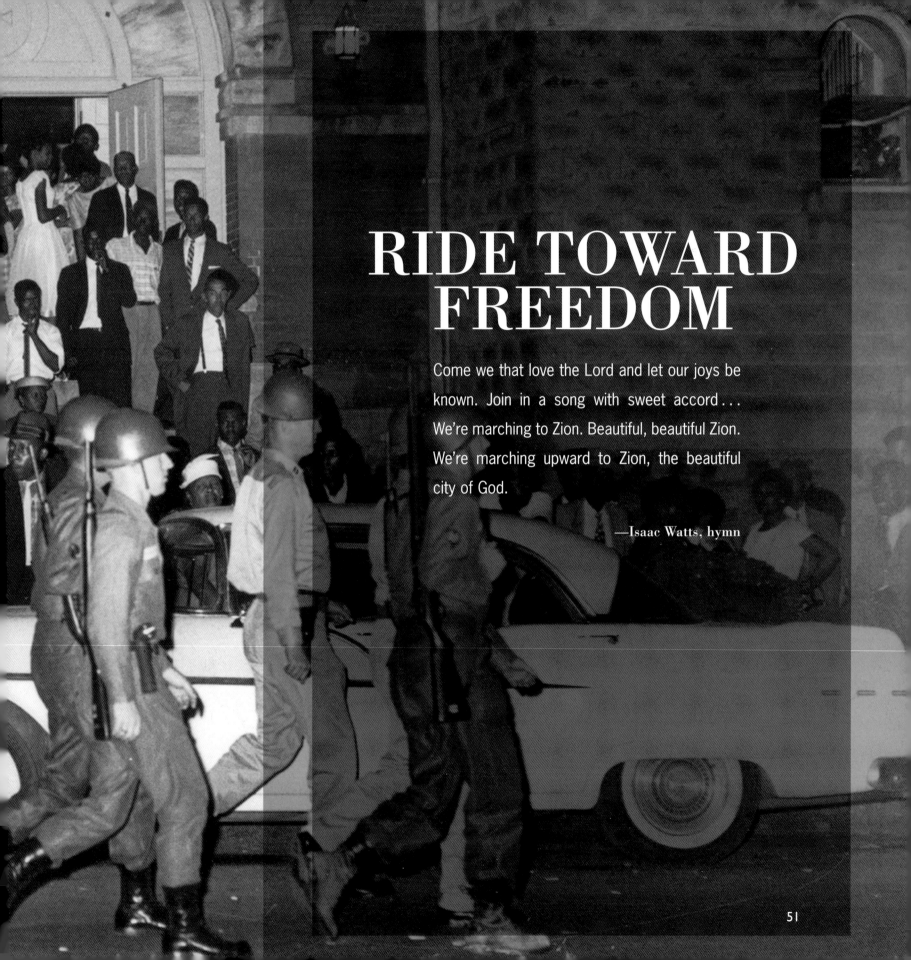

RIDE TOWARD FREEDOM

Come we that love the Lord and let our joys be known. Join in a song with sweet accord... We're marching to Zion. Beautiful, beautiful Zion. We're marching upward to Zion, the beautiful city of God.

—Isaac Watts, hymn

In January 1960, Martin and Coretta moved to Atlanta, leaving Ralph as the new president of the Montgomery Improvement Association. As his father's co-pastor at Ebenezer Baptist Church, Martin now had more time to concentrate on the development of his newly formed Southern Christian Leadership Conference (SCLC). On February 1, Joseph McNeil, Franklin McCain, Ezell Blair, and David Richmond, four black freshmen from the Negro Agricultural and Technical College, sat down at the all-white lunch counter of the F. W. Woolworth's in Greensboro, North Carolina—without the leadership of a major civil rights organization—thus beginning the national lunch counter sit-in demonstrations.

Demonstrations spread throughout the South like wildfire, challenging the Jim Crow tradition that blacks should be served only standing up. As this story unfolded, Martin was arrested and indicted for perjury by the Alabama State Income Tax Division. A jury later found him not guilty. Simultaneously, Ralph was holding prayer meetings in Montgomery for Martin, the sit-in students at Alabama State College, and the segregationists—"the oppressors." At the March 6 meeting, following the singing of "Battle Hymn of the Republic" and the national anthem, Ralph asked those gathered to pray fervently for their oppressive governor, mayor, and board of education. They then humbly prayed for the strength and courage to continue the struggle, sang the Negro national anthem, and marched into the streets of Montgomery. On March 29, the New York Committee to Defend Martin Luther King placed an advertisement in the New York Times requesting national support for Martin so that he could continue his fight for Negro voting rights, as well as for the Southern students who were protesting segregation. The advertisement was signed by noted artists and politicians, including former first lady Eleanor Roosevelt, Nat "King" Cole, Marlon Brando, Stella Adler, Harry Belafonte, and Sidney Poitier—83 in all. In addition, the names of 20 Southern black ministers were listed. All were dedicated to the nonviolent struggle for freedom in the South.

Because of their uncompromising stand for civil rights, Ralph and the Reverends S. S. Seay of Montgomery, Joseph E. Lowery of Mobile, and Fred Shuttlesworth of Birmingham—along with the New York Times—were named in five libel suits by the city of Montgomery and various Alabama officials: Governor James Patterson, Montgomery mayor Earl Hayes, Police Commissioner L. B. Sullivan, Third City Commissioner Frank Parks, and the former police commissioner. They charged that the ad caused them "ridicule and shame," but it was believed that the suit was filed to render the men defenseless and discourage the Northern newspapers from appealing to the national conscience. The ministers' automobiles were seized and sold at public auction. In addition, Ralph's farmland—which had been in his family for three generations—was auctioned off. Ralph said, "This has made my family and me more determined than ever to carry on the struggle for our democratic ideals and freedom. We may have lost our material possessions, but we have our health, our faith, and we will never give up."

On April 5, 1960, Ralph received an invitation from Kwame Nkrumah, prime minister of Ghana, to address a peace conference in Accra on the topic of "Nonviolence and the Struggle of the Negro for Positive Action for Peace and Security of Africa." Attendees at the conference included many prominent dignitaries, among them Haile Selassie of Ethiopia.

By May, the city of Atlanta was starting to show the stirrings of major racial unrest. Sit-in demonstrators had already been arrested at Union Station and various restaurants. State troopers distributed billy clubs when 2,000 Negroes tried to march to the state capitol in observance of the sixth anniversary of the desegregation of schools.

The SCLC held its convention October 12–14, 1960, in Shreveport, Louisiana. After Dr. Gardner Taylor delivered the keynote address, Ralph, Guy Carawan, director of the voter registration drive for the NAACP, and Dr. C. O. Simpkins, a local dentist, were pulled over by police while en route to their hotel in Dr. Simpkins's car. They were accused of stealing the recently purchased car. The men were taken to the police station, where officers went through Ralph's briefcase and took a sermon and Montgomery Improvement Association financial records. Upon their release, the men discovered the letters "KKK" scratched into the hood of Dr. Simpkins's car. At a freedom rally the following night, Martin told the crowd, "So many forces in our nation have served to scar the dreams of our democracy. The Ku Klux Klan, white citizen councils, and other extremist groups have scarred the dream by their fanatical acts and bitter words." He may not have known how correct he was when he said, "In the midst of this conspiracy of silence and apathy, the Negro must act. It may well be that the Negro is God's instrument to save the soul of America. The student movement has marked an era in the history of the United States." With those words, Martin joined the students at their sit-in and boycott demonstrations of Rich's Department Store. When Martin was arrested, he received a four-month sentence at Reidsville State Penitentiary for violating a suspended sentence he had received earlier for driving in Georgia with an Alabama license. Bail was denied. Thanks to a telephone call from Robert F. Kennedy, the brother of presidential candidate John F. Kennedy, Judge Mitchell of Dekalb County released Martin until his appeal could be heard by a higher court. John Kennedy later called Coretta to express his concern. A few weeks later, with the help of the Negro vote, Kennedy was elected president of the United States.

"In the years immediately following the Montgomery Bus Boycott, segregation continued on public transportation in most portions of the South. Once the Supreme Court had ruled on the question, we assumed bus lines all over the region would immediately discontinue Jim Crow seating requirements and that everyone would accept such a change, but that simply did not happen. The Southern establishment would not cooperate in seeking obedience to constitutional law; instead they used this occasion to win fleeting popularity by promising the white constituency that the Supreme Court's decision could be circumvented and the status quo maintained, despite the Constitution. It was inconceivable to them that a court decree could simply wipe out their tradition. The Southern legal establishment was saying, 'Maybe we can find some way in which our local system is different. Maybe we can find a legal loophole.' In that spirit, they devised stratagems to confound the Supreme Court, and the word went out all over the South: 'Don't give in. Just keep doing things the way we always have. This will all blow over in a few years.' Politicians such as Orval Faubus, Ross Barnett, Lester Maddox, and Bull Connor temporarily grew in popularity because of their violent confrontations against blacks. However, they would eventually lose their battle and have their names marred in history because of their racist, violent pursuits."

—RDA

In May 1961, as the result of a number of confrontations over public transportation, Attorney General Robert F. Kennedy asked the Interstate Commerce Commission to declare segregation in all public transportation facilities illegal and to force compliance with this regulation nationwide.

"Thank you, Dr. King. To the presiding officer and to my fellow soldiers in the army for freedom and first-class citizenship. It is with deep humility and grave determination that I accept this gavel, the symbol of leadership of the Montgomery Improvement Association (MIA), from the hand of my great and abiding friend, the Moses of the twentieth century. This gavel represents the longings, hopes, and aspirations of my people who just want to be free and who are determined that nothing will stop them short of first-class citizenship in all forms of American life. This gavel must be sounded here in the 'cradle of the confederacy' until the pharaohs let my people go.

"Let me set the record straight: I am not Martin Luther King. He is my closest friend and I wish not to be compared with him. Neither did I seek, nor do I ambitiously desire this high office. I have not waited until this hour to start working for the cause of freedom or with the program of the MIA. I have been with the MIA since its very conception, when it was only an idea, and shared in the conceiving of that idea. I became its first 'messenger' on December 2, 1955, and ran through the streets bearing the good news to my fellow ministers of the gospel. Even though our great leader is leaving this town, this gavel must not become silent, but it must be sounded again and again. Therefore, I shall sound it to the best of my ability. For there will be no slowing up; there will be no turning back; there will be no selling out; there will be no turning to hatred, bitterness, or violence, but there will be continued moving forward. Our goal: first-class citizenship. Our method: love and nonviolence. We want our freedom now. I cannot do this job without your support. Therefore, I call upon each of you to give your best cooperation. Just try to give to me what I have tried to give Martin Luther King. If you follow this course, I cannot promise you an easy sail. But I can promise you victory. I have been on top of the mountain and I have seen the land. There is no mistake, it is truly Canaan. Some of them tell us that we cannot enter the land but we believe 'that with the help of God we can enter the land.' But it will not be easy. We must prepare ourselves for suffering. Some of us may have to give our very lives, but this will only speed up the coming of the inevitable, so don't ask God to do away with your Gethsemane, but use it to make up your mind to drink the bitter cup. The forces of evil will now say everything bad they can about us. They will do all within their power to divide and even defeat us. They will threaten and intimidate us. They may cut off our credit and lock us up in jail. They may again bomb our homes and churches, fire us from our jobs, bruise and beat our bodies, take our very lives, but none of this must turn us around. We must keep moving toward freedom. We have a date with destiny. And a rendezvous with justice. So don't ask God to remove the cross, for if there is no cross then there can be no crown. Regardless to how dark it gets, we must keep moving. Remember, Easter always follows Good Friday, and after dark comes the dawn. We must keep moving not for our sake alone, but for the sake of America and its position of leadership in the world. We must keep moving for the sake of the kingdom of God. We represent eternity. Our forefathers died in the faith that if we keep inching and inching along, we'd get there by and by. I cannot turn around, for eternity pulls at my soul. So I step out into the future, knowing not what it holds, but knowing God, who holds the future. I shall be free someday."

—RDA
Acceptance speech as president of the
Montgomery Improvement Association
February 1, 1960

The Freedom Riders
May 14, 1961
Anniston, Alabama

In order to test the South's compliance with the new regulation prohibiting segregation in all public transportation facilities, the Congress of Racial Equality (CORE) dispatched two biracial groups due south from Washington, D.C., on Greyhound and Trailways buses. The first group rode without any major incidents until they arrived at the closed Greyhound bus depot in Anniston, Alabama. The awaiting crowd of nearly 200 became an angry mob as the bus came to a stop and the passengers tried to disembark. The mob hurled rocks, slashed a tire, and smashed windows. The bus tried to get away, but it was chased by the mob until a flat tire forced it to stop six miles outside of Anniston. The mob surrounded the bus, smashed the rest of the windows, and tossed in a firebomb, setting the vehicle ablaze. Smoke and flames forced the Freedom Riders from the bus. Twelve people were treated at the hospital and the bus was completely destroyed.

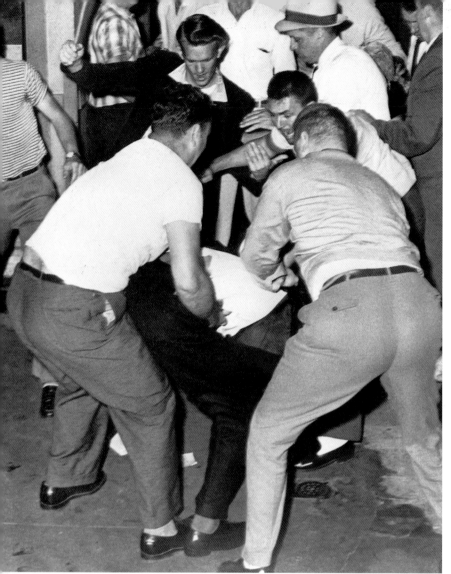

Montgomery, May 20, 1961

Under the watchful eye of presidential emissary John Seigenthaler, the Freedom Riders rode into Montgomery, where an irate mob viciously attacked Seigenthaler and both black and white riders for "race mixing." Horrified by what they saw, Fred and Anna Gaches, a white Montgomery couple who happened to be near the station, begged the police—who were standing around watching—to stop the beating. The mob and police threatened the Gacheses for trying to defend the defenseless Freedom Riders, and the couple was arrested and jailed on charges of disorderly conduct. There were other whites on the street that day who were outraged by what they saw, but unlike the Gacheses, they lacked the courage to speak up, and watched in silence as women and men were beaten nearly to death.

(Below) Bloodied students John Lewis of the Nashville Christian Leadership Conference and James Zwerg, an exchange student from Fisk University. (Opposite) Zwerg waited in the street for more than an hour for a Negro ambulance to take him to the Negro St. Jude's Hospital because the white ambulances refused to help him.

Birmingham, May 14, 1961

A savage mob was waiting at the Trailways station in Birmingham for the second bus to arrive. It was Mother's Day, so the police did not make an appearance until after the vicious mob had beaten the Freedom Riders with lead pipes. Cries of "Hit him!" rang out as a fist repeatedly punched Charles Person in the face, forcing him to the ground. One member of the gang held him up so that others could continue to kick him. (Above) James Peck, a white Freedom Rider, intervened on Person's behalf, only to be beaten mercilessly as well. He eventually required 50 stitches. Trapped in Birmingham for hours because the bus drivers refused to take them as passengers, the Freedom Riders were forced to try and fly out of town. One airplane canceled its flight, and another was emptied by a bomb threat as it prepared to depart.

Montgomery—First Baptist Church
May 21, 1961

John Lewis and the other Freedom Riders later met at the Abernathy home to discuss their plans. The Abernathy parsonage could accommodate only a few Riders overnight, so Ralph found additional housing for the others among his First Baptist congregation. Afterward, he called and invited Martin to come from Atlanta to attend a mass meeting at First Baptist that evening.

While the mass meeting was going on inside the church, the belligerent mob reappeared, violently overturning a car, setting it on fire, and threatening to harm anyone who emerged from the church. Ralph, Martin, the Freedom Riders, and hundreds of well-wishers were trapped overnight in First Baptist. Outraged by the beatings and the failure of the police to maintain peace, Attorney General Robert F. Kennedy began a nightlong negotiation with Governor Patterson to ensure the safety of those trapped inside the church.

Unable to reach an amicable agreement, Kennedy sent in the National Guard. In retaliation, the embittered Alabama governor declared martial law. Patterson said that "the same federal marshalls who escorted King into the state should take him back out."

Early the following morning, the National Guard arrived and released the captive people from the church. For those who didn't have transportation, the Guard drove them to their neighborhoods in the back of military vehicles.

(Left) Martin and Ralph took turns sleeping and waiting for the phone call from the Justice Department ensuring their safety.

(Top) People were forced to sleep on the overcrowded, hard wooden pews.

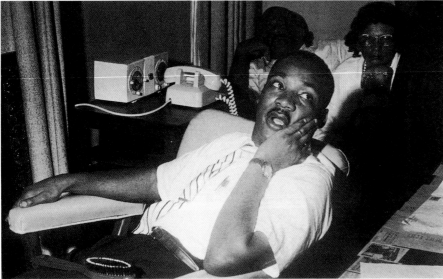

(Opposite) Beginning May 24, the National Guard and state troopers patrolled the Greyhound and Trailways bus terminals for several days following the rioting. Inside the Trailways terminal, Freedom Riders prepared to board the bus under heavy guard. While waiting in the overcrowded waiting rooms, blacks integrated the white lunch counter for the first time in the history of Alabama. Because of the national press attention and the presence of the Justice Department and the National Guard, Alabama whites pretended to ignore tradition, and served the Freedom Riders. The bus was escorted down Highway 80 by the National Guard.

The following morning, Ralph, Martin, and John Lewis held a press conference at the Abernathy parsonage to announce the continuation of the Freedom Rides.

(Left) One day later, Ralph and Bernard Lee (in glasses), a student activist from Alabama State, were arrested along with three white college professors for integrating the very same lunch counter.

Desegregation of Universities and Public Libraries

In 1954, the U.S. Supreme Court overruled the "separate but equal" clause in *Brown v. Board of Education,* thus allowing for school integration. Autherine Lucy was the first black to gain admission to the University of Alabama at Tuscaloosa in 1956. Miss Lucy was suspended, however, when students rioted against her. On January 10, 1961, Charlayne Hunter (later Hunter-Gault) and Hamilton Holmes integrated the University of Georgia at Athens. On their second day at school, Hunter (left) and Holmes were withdrawn by the administration for their "own protection" because of the fierce threat of violence from white students. Public libraries were also segregated. However, in the fall of 1961, James Meredith, with the assistance of federal troops ordered by President Kennedy, entered the University of Mississippi against the wishes of Governor Ross Barnett. Whites rioted, leaving two people dead—but Meredith continued to study at the university until he graduated in 1963.

Atlanta, Georgia

After Martin moved to Atlanta in 1960, he called Ralph daily, asking him to consider moving there as well. But Ralph and Juanita loved First Baptist, and Alabama was our home.

"There is another real problem," Ralph said. "It is the community. The students of Alabama State College are depending on me to give them advice and support in the struggle and their problems caused by the 'sit-in' demonstrations. The community is in turmoil. The city is in a police state. Negroes are experiencing more brutal treatment from the police department than they ever have in recent times. Martin has left town now and these people are looking to me. Must I leave them in this hour of trial and go to Atlanta?"

Martin, however, was persistent. He and his father found a lovely church in Atlanta for Ralph to pastor—West Hunter Street Baptist Church. Its former pastor, the Rev. A. F. Fisher, had suddenly died, and Martin asked them to consider calling Ralph. After Ralph preached a trial sermon, Deacon J. R. Butts, chairman of the Deacon Board, offered him the position on June 13, 1961. But Juanita was deeply saddened, and begged Ralph to stay in Montgomery. She didn't know anyone in Atlanta except the King family and feared that her life might be lonely. Despite Ralph's love for Alabama, and because of his love for his closest friend, he eventually said yes. On November 5, 1961, Ralph ended his ministry at First Baptist, and on February 11, 1962, Martin moved us to Atlanta, and our lives changed forever.

The day that the moving van came to take us away, Juanita cried. Quietly, she said good-bye to Rosa Coleman, our beloved housekeeper and friend, and then walked among her rosebushes. As we drove away, my doll fell from my hands to the ground, a part of my innocence left behind in Montgomery.

(Opposite and top) Installation services at West Hunter Street Baptist Church. As the installation preacher, Martin administered the oath of office to Ralph. Dr. Benjamin E. Mays, president of Morehouse College, was the speaker for the installation banquet, and the Rev. S. S. Seay of Montgomery was the guest minister. Rev. M. L. King Sr. was seated on the right side of the pulpit. Mrs. A. F. Fisher presided.

(Bottom) Ralph arrives at Atlanta's airport.

(Following pages) The Abernathys and the Kings.

69

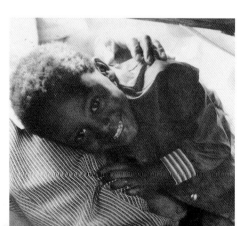  

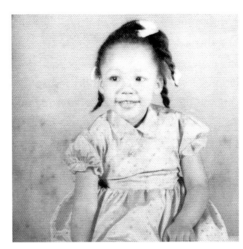

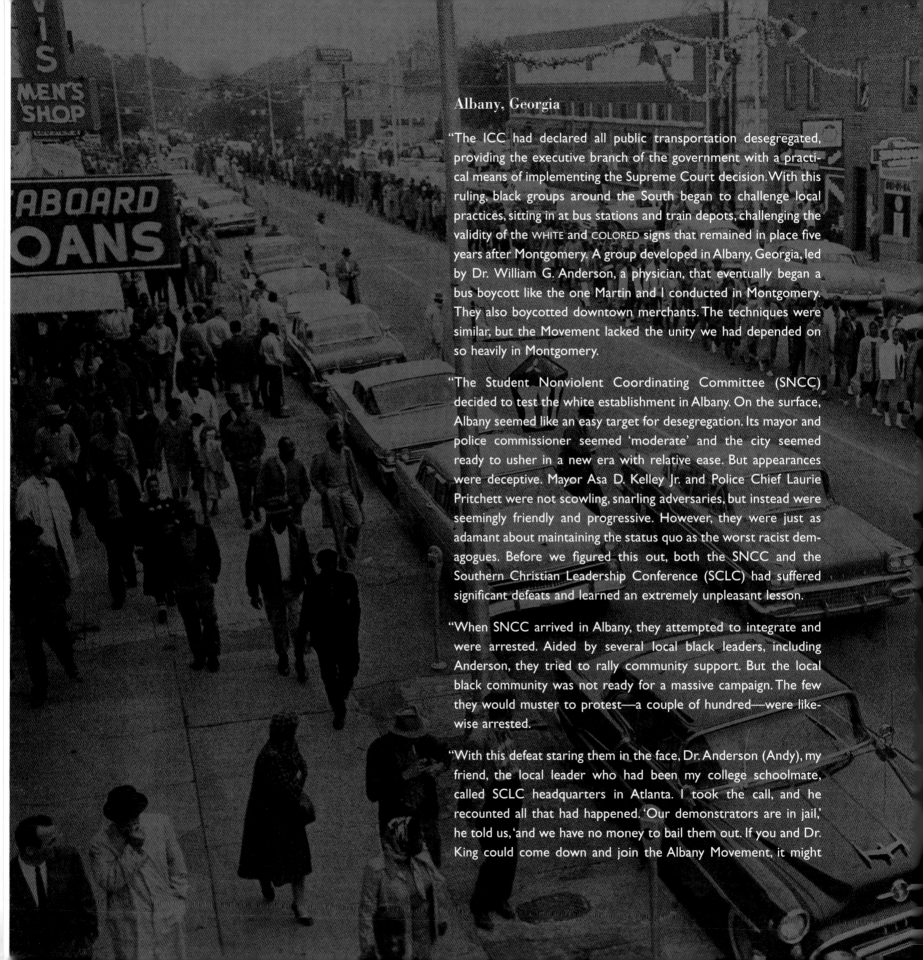

Albany, Georgia

"The ICC had declared all public transportation desegregated, providing the executive branch of the government with a practical means of implementing the Supreme Court decision. With this ruling, black groups around the South began to challenge local practices, sitting in at bus stations and train depots, challenging the validity of the WHITE and COLORED signs that remained in place five years after Montgomery. A group developed in Albany, Georgia, led by Dr. William G. Anderson, a physician, that eventually began a bus boycott like the one Martin and I conducted in Montgomery. They also boycotted downtown merchants. The techniques were similar, but the Movement lacked the unity we had depended on so heavily in Montgomery.

"The Student Nonviolent Coordinating Committee (SNCC) decided to test the white establishment in Albany. On the surface, Albany seemed like an easy target for desegregation. Its mayor and police commissioner seemed 'moderate' and the city seemed ready to usher in a new era with relative ease. But appearances were deceptive. Mayor Asa D. Kelley Jr. and Police Chief Laurie Pritchett were not scowling, snarling adversaries, but instead were seemingly friendly and progressive. However, they were just as adamant about maintaining the status quo as the worst racist demagogues. Before we figured this out, both the SNCC and the Southern Christian Leadership Conference (SCLC) had suffered significant defeats and learned an extremely unpleasant lesson.

"When SNCC arrived in Albany, they attempted to integrate and were arrested. Aided by several local black leaders, including Anderson, they tried to rally community support. But the local black community was not ready for a massive campaign. The few they would muster to protest—a couple of hundred—were likewise arrested.

"With this defeat staring them in the face, Dr. Anderson (Andy), my friend, the local leader who had been my college schoolmate, called SCLC headquarters in Atlanta. I took the call, and he recounted all that had happened. 'Our demonstrators are in jail,' he told us, 'and we have no money to bail them out. If you and Dr. King could come down and join the Albany Movement, it might

rally more local people and attract some financial help to get these young people out of jail.' Martin returned the next day and I told him about Dr. Anderson's call. 'What do you think we should do?' he asked. 'I think we should go,' I said, 'but maybe we should send somebody down to look over the place first, just to see what to expect.'

"A couple of our staff drove down to Albany to question the black community and determine how much support we could expect from them. They were immediately arrested, so we never got a full scouting report. After Martin talked to Dr. Anderson, we decided to go down ourselves.

"The more the black demonstrators gathered, the more adamant the mayor and the commissioners became. Instead of weakening, the white leaders seemed to be gaining strength. The reason for this growing support was the local newspaper, the *Albany Herald*, which was edited by a fierce defender of segregation. The *Herald* denounced the members of SNCC, and later Martin and me, as 'professional agitators,' suggesting that we were an army of mercenaries who had come to tear up the city. That charge was to be repeated over the years, often with the out-and-out accusation that we were paid by the Communist party, which was a blatant lie. We were never Communist or Socialist.

"When we got to Albany, we discovered the black community—and more particularly, the black demonstrators—divided. The organizations participating in the campaign had agreed to merge their identity into one group called the 'Albany Movement,' and to be governed by a steering committee. But by the time we arrived, the unity they had achieved had collapsed. Everyone had a different strategy. Everyone wanted to be in charge.

"Dr. Anderson, a man of remarkable patience, was beset from all sides. The Movement had already made demands of the city that had been in part rejected, though at one point they seemed to have been near agreement. The U.S. Department of Justice was leaning on Mayor Kelley in an effort to bring the whole matter to a satisfactory and nonviolent conclusion.

"We held mass meetings that night at Shiloh and Mt. Zion Baptist. Since the churches were directly across from each other, we addressed the crowd in both places. I spoke first, then Martin, and finally Dr. Anderson. Martin and I were able to bring their temperatures to a boil with calls to sacrifice and action. The building was trembling with cheers. Andy was delighted, and in his final words, Dr. Anderson called for the marchers to assemble the next day for a protest march into downtown Albany.

"The next morning we drove down to Shiloh Baptist Church and found a moderate crowd waiting there, perhaps three or four hundred. There were no signs of policemen, and for the first time it appeared as if the Albany Movement would mount a march without massive arrests. But, of course, we had to see what Mayor Kelley's response would be.

"Ten o'clock came and went without reply. Finally at around noon a hand-carried letter arrived from Mayor Kelley rejecting the demand and accusing Dr. Anderson of betraying an agreement to work through already established negotiators."

—RDA

77

With the coming spring, Martin and Ralph took their message to the streets. Since it was mostly women who attended mass meetings, they had to go to places where black men would congregate—such as pool halls and other open areas—to teach the message of peace and nonviolence. Likewise, Juanita went to a Quaker retreat in Lake Geneva, Wisconsin, to speak about the struggles in Albany, and Coretta helped supervise the Albany office with Wyatt T. Walker. The efforts of everyone were needed to ensure success in Albany.

On December 16, 1961, Martin, Ralph, and Dr. William Anderson (light suit) were arrested, along with 266 Negroes, for parading without a permit. They were accompanied to jail by Coretta and Juanita. At a press conference after his release, Ralph called on President Kennedy to issue a "second emancipation proclamation" because of the arrest three days earlier of 60 student demonstrators who were praying in front of City Hall for a just verdict in the hearing of the 11 Freedom Riders.

(Opposite) Recruiting movement officers in a pool hall in Albany.

(Above) Shady Grove Baptist Church, the headquarters of the Southern Christian Leadership Conference (SCLC) Voter Registration Drive in Leesburg, Georgia, was destroyed by an explosion and fire on August 15, 1962. Martin charged that the bombing was deliberate, but local investigators said they found no evidence of explosives or arson.

(Above) Former Brooklyn Dodger Jackie Robinson (right) went to Albany to inspect the ruins of another bombed church and to help raise $30,000 to rebuild the church. Rabbi Israel Dressner arrived from Springfield, New Jersey, to offer his services as well.

(Opposite) On August 24, 1962, Ralph and Martin, preoccupied with the church bombings in Albany, exit the funeral services of Cleveland Lyons, a member of Ebenezer. They are followed by Rev. M. L. King Sr. and Rev. William Holmes Borders.

As racial tensions in the South kept mounting, Martin met with Bobby Kennedy (above, with SCLC vice president C. O. Simpkins) to discuss the crisis and the need for blacks to have the right to vote. "President Kennedy won our deepest respect after he telephoned Coretta when Martin was arrested," Juanita said. "He was sympathetic to our needs." Bobby Kennedy later issued a statement: "I find it wholly inexplicable why the city council of Albany will not sit down with the citizens of Albany, who may be Negroes, and attempt to secure them, in a peaceful way, their rights. The U.S. government is involved in sitting down in Geneva with the Soviet Union. I can't understand why the government of Albany cannot do the same for American citizens."

(Opposite) On December 17, 1962, the president invited Martin to the White House to meet with the American Negro Leadership on Africa. Also at the meeting was the U.S. delegate to the United Nations, Ambassador Adlai E. Stevenson (center).

The history of Birmingham was ugly and the potential for community violence exceeded all other Southern cities. 'Bummingham' was known as the most segregated city this side of Johannesburg, South Africa. Having just returned from Albany, Birmingham offered us the opportunity to redeem ourselves and proved that the Southern Christian Leadership Conference (SCLC) was truly a national organization, that we were the spearhead of the Civil Rights Movement. Birmingham was hard, mean, and run by an unbending white establishment, perfectly symbolized by the steel statue that towered over the city, holding up a torch. We knew that the unprecedented bombings we had experienced at the end of the Montgomery boycott were relatively common occurrences in Birmingham and required no extraordinary tensions to set them off. Middle-class blacks, such as our attorney, Arthur Shores, lived in a part of town nicknamed 'Dynamite Hill.' Ku Klux Klan members disliked Shores because he was the first black lawyer in the history of the state and he played golf regularly in Jamaica, a thought that used to drive them wild with envy.

"As Birmingham was a major Southern industrial city, racial, ethnic, and economic animosities were easily provoked by the lower working-class whites toward blacks. Given the history of the South, equality annoyed working-class whites, who dignified themselves by claiming their social and economic superiority to blacks. With equal pay for equal work, they had no grounds for their 'self-proclaimed' superiority.

"Theophilus Eugene 'Bull' Connor was legendary in the state of Alabama. He was a shrewd and bold adversary in a fight. We could expect maximum effort on his part, if he were elected mayor (a distinct possibility). It would mean a city united in defense of Jim Crow.

"The black leadership of Birmingham under Fred Shuttlesworth was not supported by most of the black clergy. They were willing to wait, typical of the crowd that had gained some prosperity and credibility in the white community. Since helping the Freedom Riders, Fred had operated without support, except among college students. He was courageous, knew what had to be done and was willing to do it regardless of the risks.

"In the summer of 1962, Shuttlesworth led a series of demonstrations in an attempt to persuade downtown Birmingham stores to integrate their facilities and staffs. The merchants expressed some willingness to cooperate, but they told Shuttlesworth and the Alabama Christian Movement for Human Rights that they could not integrate their stores as long as the city government objected. When they said this, everybody knew they were really talking about the man they called 'Bull.' Shuttlesworth, who had joined us during Montgomery, came to an SCLC retreat and formally asked us to intervene in Birmingham. He wanted us to help him integrate Birmingham's public accommodations. We had been considering the possibility for a long time, along with a number of options; but at this meeting we all knew we were going to make a decision which would irrevocably commit us to the venture. To win in Birmingham might well be to win in the rest of the nation. The people of Birmingham needed us more than anyone else did at that time.

"After we had decided to commit ourselves to Birmingham, we considered the matter of timing. Under ordinary circumstances we might have gone in a little earlier, but the upcoming election affected our strategy and made us quite willing to hold off. Bull Connor announced that he would run for mayor under the new charter.

At this point, we were poised on the border, waiting to invade; but we knew that we couldn't run the risk of ending in our advance team to scout the area and recruit protesters. The rumor of coming demonstrations would panic the white voters and perhaps cause them to vote for a man with police experience rather than the more businesslike Albert Boutwell. We would be much safer facing a government headed by Albert Boutwell than one headed by Bull Connor.

It's important to understand the national political context in which Birmingham took place. The Supreme Court had cleared only limited ground. President Kennedy's Civil Rights Bill was still in its developmental stages, and it was generally assumed that discrimination in public accommodations would be taken care of by the legislative branch, at the initiation of the president. In the second year of his term, Kennedy became more and more interested in civil rights legislation, not just because he wanted to, but because he believed that he had to.

Money was always a problem because SCLC was run on contributions of thousands of people, black and white, who believed in our cause. We used the money for transportation, literature, legal fees, fines, and for the posting of bonds in case of arrests. Martin and I never received salaries, and the Reverend James Lawson, a local leader in Memphis, was unsalaried like the two of us. But our regular staff, Wyatt T. Walker, Andy Young, James Bevel, Hosea Williams, Bernard Lee, Randolph Blackwell, L. D. Reddick, Dorothy Cotton, and Septima Clark, were all on the payroll. Whenever we entered a new city, we would also hire additional staff members as needed. In Birmingham we hired several

Outstanding people, including James Orange and an extraordinary man, Ben Owens, whom we called 'Sunshine.'

"On April 2, 1963, Albert Boutwell defeated Bull Connor by a substantial margin in the mayoral election. So, April 3, Martin and I flew to Birmingham to begin our campaign.

"We decided to appoint an advisory board of prominent black business and professional leaders, knowing that while they might not be active, they would serve On Good Friday, they advised us no to march to City Hall or demonstrate for our rights. We met at the Gaston Motel to plan strategy, and while ou advisory board warned us against the march, across the street in the 16th Street Baptist Church our waiting supporters were singing hymns. Outside hundreds and hundreds of people milled about, waiting two hours fo word to march. As we talked in the motel, two white policemen sat in the church with what I called the 'doohicky bug,' a transmitter tha beamed everything that was said to Bull Connor, sitting in Police Headquarters a few blocks away. Suddenly Martin had enough. 'Ralph,' he said 'I'm going to march regardless of wha they say. But Sunday is Easter, and you're the only preacher at Wes Hunter.' Then he reached out and embraced me. I knew what he was thinking: he might eithe be arrested and jailed for months, or else be killed. He was giving me a way out. 'Martin,' I said, 'what are you trying to say to me?' I smiled and shook my head. 'If you're going to march, then I'm going to march, too.' 'Okay,' he said, 'then let's go.' He turned to the assembled advisors, and he said 'Gentlemen, thank you for your words of advice, but we're going to have to march now.'"

The Good Friday March

Ralph and Martin, dressed in dungarees to dramatize their boycott of department stores, asked that people boycott stores that not only refused to allow Negroes to use their facilities, but also those that would not employ blacks. Without the economic strength of the Negro dollar at Easter, businesses would suffer great financial losses; this would force merchants to address the Negroes' concerns. In direct violation of a court order banning marches, boycotts, and demonstrations—and against the advice of the upper-middle-class black businessmen and clergymen—Martin and Ralph led what became known as the Good Friday March. After allowing them to walk for eight blocks, Bull Connor ordered his men to arrest them. They were hauled off by policemen clutching the backs of their pants.

"Holding each of us by the seat of our pants, they propelled us toward a waiting paddywagon, lifted us in the air, and tossed us inside like a couple of sacks into darkness. We could hear shouts and screams, mingled with the roar of motorcycles and the screech of tires. Massive arrests were taking place. Then we heard voices drawing closer—three men. One we recognized as the voice of a man we had yet to meet—Bull Connor. 'Where's Martin Luther King and Ralph Abernathy?' he said in a hoarse growl, less than two feet away outside the wagon. 'Right there inside,' said a second voice. 'We got them both.' 'Well, let's arrest them all and take everybody off to the jailhouse,' said Connor. 'What jailhouse?' said a third voice. 'The Birmingham jail is full. The Bessemer jail is full. The Jefferson County jail is full. The fairground is full.' There was a long pause. 'OK,' Connor shouted, 'Don't arrest another goddamn nigger.' 'What about King and Abernathy?' the first voice asked. 'Take them to the Jefferson County jail. And make sure they double up a couple of the other prisoners so there are two empty cells. These two have never been separated. Let's see if they can get along without one another for a change. Put them in solitary.' But Connor had made a strategic error. Left to brood, Martin had read a letter in the local newspaper signed by Catholic, Protestant, and Jewish religious leaders, telling us to go home. Fired up, he wrote on scraps of paper and toilet tissue his *Letter from Birmingham Jail*. This document aroused people all over the country. It will be read by Americans long after Bull Connor has ceased to be a footnote to history."

—RDA

Excerpts of the *Letter from Birmingham Jail*, April 16, 1963

My Dear Fellow Clergymen:

I cannot sit idly by in Atlanta and not be concerned about what happens in Birmingham. Injustice anywhere is a threat to justice everywhere.... We had no alternative except to prepare for direct action, whereby we would present our very bodies as a means of laying our case before the conscience of the local and the national community.... Nonviolent direct action seeks to create such a crisis and foster such a tension that a community which has constantly refused to negotiate is forced to confront the issue...which is necessary for growth...freedom is never voluntarily given by the oppressor; it must be demanded by the oppressed...it is easy for those who have never felt the stinging dark of segregation to say, "Wait." But when you have seen vicious mobs lynch your mothers and fathers, when you have seen hate-filled policemen curse, kick, and even kill your black brothers and sisters; when you see the vast majority of your twenty million Negro brothers smothering in an airtight cage of poverty in the midst of an affluent society...when your first name becomes "nigger," your middle name becomes "boy"... and your wife and mother are never given the respected title "Mrs."—when you are harried by day and haunted by night, plagued with inner fears and outer resentments...then you will understand why we find it difficult to wait...Oppressed people cannot remain oppressed forever. The yearning for freedom eventually manifests itself, and that is what has happened to the American Negro. Something within has reminded him of his birthright of freedom....Try to understand why....One day the South will know that these disinherited children were in reality standing up for what is best in the American dream and for the most sacred values in our Judeo-Christian heritage...dug deep by the founding fathers in their formulations of the Constitution and the Declaration of Independence. If I have said anything in this letter that overstates the truth, I beg you to forgive me. If I have said anything that understates the truth and indicates my having a patience that allows me to settle for anything less than brotherhood, I beg God to forgive me. Yours for the cause of Peace and Brotherhood,

—MLK

The Birmingham Fire Department lay in wait for the young demonstrators to march into their midst while Martin and Ralph were still in the custody of the Birmingham Police.

"The force of the water hoses directed at the children was so great that I saw it peel the bark off a tree."

—Glenn E. Smiley

"Today I stood on Holy ground. I stood on Holy ground in this church. . . . I saw young men and women come running in with their garments torn from them, and their bodies bleeding because they had been bitten by the dogs. I saw little children come running in with water dripping from their bodies and from their garments, and I said, 'This is Holy ground.' And God said to me, 'Abernathy, pull off your shoes.' It won't be long now, before America will be the land of the free and the home of the brave. I saw those children, I saw those young people as they violated the orders of their school principals. I saw them steal away from their classrooms, marching toward city hall. And I said, this is D Day. But it won't be long before we'll have V Day—Victory Day!

"Where Negroes can be bitten by dogs; where Negroes can have the firehoses turned on us, have us knocked down and still not turn around. I'll tell you what they said today when they came into the church, they are going back out there. And when they turn the water hoses back on, 'we are gonna lay down so they won't have to knock us down' . . .

"Talk about a pilgrimage . . . I want you to know that they are looking to Birmingham, because you have started something. We've got a straight line to the White House. And we want to hear from the White House. If Bull Connor will not do it, if Governor Wallace won't do it, then Bobby Kennedy will!!!

"Are you for Freedom tonight? I told you last night that I speak with authority. But these reporters don't believe me. They think I'm just a rabble-rouser. But I speak with every Negro in 16th Street backing me up tonight. I speak with every Negro in Birmingham who is in his right mind, backing me up tonight. DO YOU WANT FREEDOM? IF YOU WANT FREEDOM . . . SAY FREEDOM! FREEDOM! FREEDOM! FREEDOM!"

—RDA, 16th Street Baptist Church

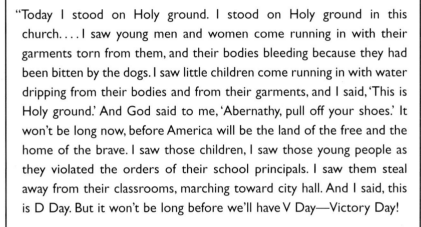

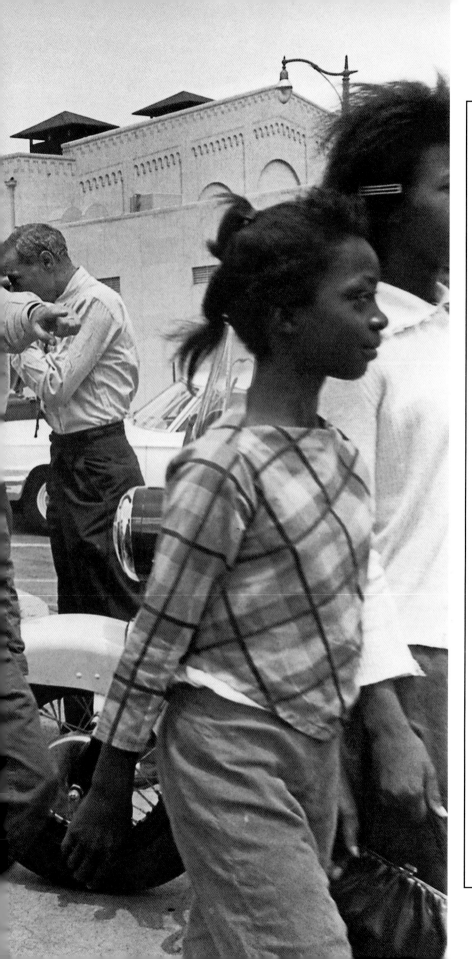

"I have had many experiences in my relatively young life. But I have never in my life had an experience like I am now having in Birmingham, Alabama. This is the most inspiring movement that has ever taken place in the United States of America. Never in the history of this nation have so many people been arrested for the cause of freedom and human dignity. You know there are approximately twenty-five hundred people in jail right now. . . . The thing that we are challenged to do is to keep this Movement moving. There is power in unity and there is power in numbers. As long as we keep moving like we are moving, the power structure of Birmingham will have to give in. And we are probably nearer to a solution of this problem than we are able to realize. And don't worry about your children. They are gonna be alright. Don't hold them back if they want to go to jail. For they are doing a job not only for themselves but for all of America and for all mankind.

"Somewhere we read . . . a little child shall lead them. These young people are about their father's business, and they are carving a tunnel of hope through the great mountain of despair. And they will bring to this nation a newness and a genuine quality and an idealism that it so desperately needs. And we are gonna see that they are treated right and go on and not only fill up the jails around here, but just fill up the jails all over the state of Alabama if necessary. Now there are those who would love for us to use violence. They would be happy. Governor Wallace would rear back in his comfortable chair in the state house in Montgomery, with great joy throbbing throughout his heart and his being. If we turn to violence, Mr. Connor would be delighted. Why? Because they could use this as an opportunity to say we are inciting a riot. And they would bring the state militia in here. They would have martial law declared and everything else. But if we go on with a power of unarmed truth we will be able to keep them disarmed. They just don't know what to do."

—MLK
16th Street Baptist Church

"We chatted with the press for awhile and then left for the airport. Minutes after we rounded the corner, leaving the Gaston Motel behind, a bomb exploded and blew our suite into a pile of powdered plaster and splintered wood. Had we lingered for any length of time we would most certainly have been killed in the blast. No one had the slightest doubt that the explosion was intended to kill us."

—RDA

The house of A. D. King, Martin's brother, was also bombed that same evening, though he and his family were not at home. The bombings alarmed President Kennedy. For the first time he appeared on television to address the nation about civil rights, and announced that he had called the Alabama National Guard to stand by and dispatched the army to an area near Birmingham, just in case violence spread in the city. Martin and Ralph returned to Birmingham as soon as word reached them about the bombing.... Moving around Birmingham's black neighborhoods, they assured everyone that a nonviolent victory was within their grasp, if the people would restrain themselves. They listened—though Ralph, Martin, and A.D. could see anger burning in their eyes.

Angry blacks gathered to protest the Gaston Hotel bombing. The result: a major riot—a far cry from the peaceful, nonviolent demonstrations. Bull Connor rode in his white tank to watch the buildings burn.

"During an earlier confrontation, Connor had again deployed his team of firemen, armed with hoses. At the height of the frenzy, with the two thousand lined up against him, Connor screamed to the firemen, 'Turn the hoses on them!' Hearing that cry, all of the demonstrators knelt and began to pray. The firemen stared at them, astonished by what they saw. 'Turn on those goddamned hoses!' Connor shouted. But again, the firemen refused to obey the order. The sight of people kneeling in prayer spoke more eloquently than Connor's authority. Suddenly, in the face of genuine Christian witness, he was powerless to make his own men obey him. It was a moment of revelation that might have epitomized the entire meaning of the Civil Rights Movement."

—RDA

(Above) Fred Shuttlesworth, Ralph, and Martin on their way to a press conference. Martin had great faith in the negotiated peace agreements that would halt demonstrations.

(Opposite) Defiant Alabama governor George Wallace, determined to stop the integration of schools, personally blocked the door in an attempt to stop U.S. Attorney General Katzenbach from enrolling Vivian Malone and James Hood into the University of Alabama.

Jackson, Mississippi

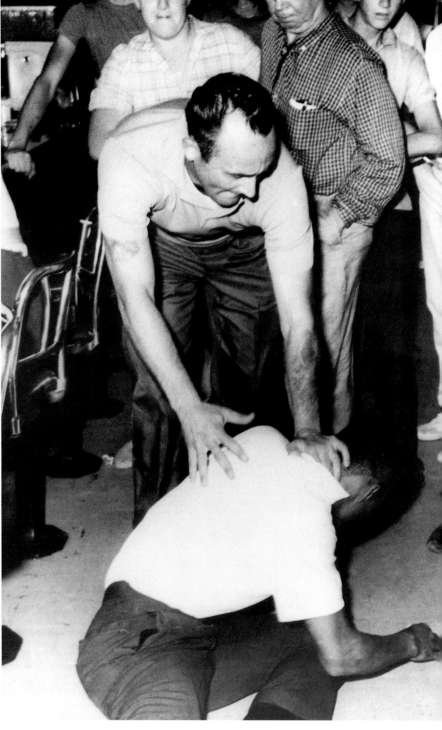

(Above, top left) In their nonviolent effort to integrate the lunch counters of Mississippi, black and white students had sugar, mustard, and ketchup poured on their heads by segregationist teenagers. (Above right) A black demonstrator, Memphis Norman, is pulled from the counter and beaten by former Jackson policeman Benny Oliver. (Above, bottom left) Inspired by Birmingham's movement, the Negroes of Jackson marched and demonstrated against the city's racial policies. Club-swinging policemen surrounded and arrested demonstrators by the hundreds, then hauled them away in city trucks to the fairgrounds, where temporary jails were set up to accommodate the overflow.

The Murder of Medgar Evers

On June 12, 1963, NAACP executive secretary Medgar Evers (top) was brutally shot and killed in his driveway (left) after returning home from a NAACP rally. His wife, Myrlie, and their children helplessly watched him die.

(Above) Three days later, Ralph, Martin, and Roy Wilkins, the national executive director of the NAACP, participated in Evers's funeral march in Jackson, Mississippi.

The March on Washington, August 28, 1963

They arrived in droves by bus along Constitution Avenue. By sunup, thousands were congregating and singing on the grassy slopes from the Lincoln Memorial Mall to the Washington Monument. That morning's program was emceed by actor Ossie Davis. Beautiful actress Ruby Dee recited "Let a race of men now rise up and take control!" Joan Baez sang "We'll Walk Hand in Hand, Someday," and Odetta brought the spiritual "Before I'll Be a Slave, I'll Be Buried in My Grave and Go Home to My Lord and Be Free." At about 10:45, A. Philip Randolph's 90,000 marchers started to arrive, and Lena Horne cried out, "Freedom!" Fred Shuttlesworth spoke, then Josephine Baker, who flew in from Paris wearing a French soldier's uniform declared, "The whole world is behind you . . . salt and pepper."

It was hot that August day in 1963 on the steps of the Lincoln Memorial. My little legs had had difficulty walking through the crowd on the Mall and climbing those steep stairs to the monument. I had never seen so many different people before in my life. There was a great euphoria of music and laughter in the air. An elderly gentleman seated at the base of the statue of Lincoln called me over to him. His face seemed familiar. He briefly tried to talk to me about the importance of the day. I told him that my father and Uncle Martin had gone to jail several times for our freedom, and now I was in Washington to do my part. I asked him his name and he said, "Benjamin Mays." He was the president of Morehouse College, a prestigious, all-male university. After we talked, I ran around aimlessly for a few more moments, smiling at my old friend, and then, feeling quite guilty for playing and enjoying myself on such an important day, I quietly took my seat in the sun on the monument steps.

To the left of me were the movie stars who had come to lend their support. I had seen some of their faces in the old movies my grandmother would let us watch with her. I would dress up in costumes, acting out the stories I had created. That afternoon at the March on Washington I knew that when I grew up, I would still play dress-up and make-believe by becoming a movie actor, and remain true to my convictions as a Freedom Fighter, too. Even though I loved my father dearly and wanted to be just like him, his work with Uncle Martin was very dangerous, and extremely frightening. Already, I was afraid to go to sleep at night, thinking that they might bomb our house again. And every evening, during supper, the telephone would ring with death threats for my mother. Dinnertime became the most dreaded hour of the day. The cruel realities of racial hatred perplexed me as a child, and the sacrifices of the Civil Rights Movement were already taking a toll on me.

Ralph Bunche, Dick Gregory, and Sammy Davis Jr. all took their turns speaking. But A. Philip Randolph brought the people to their feet, and the crowd, which included Senator Hubert Humphrey, former first lady Eleanor Roosevelt, and the senatorial delegation, chanted, "Pass the Bill!" Speakers thanked the Civil Rights women for their contributions—Rosa Parks, Daisy Bates, Diane Nash, Gloria Richardson—and Mrs. Medgar Evers and Mrs. Herbert Lee for their slain husbands. Clergyman Carson Blake apologized for the persecution of black people, and John Lewis of the Student Nonviolent Coordinating Committee angrily replied, "It is too little, too late." Walter Reuther, president of the United Auto Workers, demanded "jobs for every American." Floyd McKissick of the Congress of Racial Equality (CORE) brought words from CORE founder James Farmer, who was in a Mississippi jail. Then came Rabbi Uri Miller, Whitney Young of the Urban League, and Roy Wilkins. "I've been 'buked and I've been scorned," wailed Mahalia Jackson in her deep, soulful voice. Rabbi Joachim Prinz, president of the American Jewish Congress, declared the great shame of "a nation of silent onlookers." When Uncle Martin said, "I have a dream. A dream deeply rooted in the American dream," even I understood. We were the only children on the steps that day, that I can remember, because his children were not there. So when he proclaimed, "My four little children," I stood up and cheered for my friends. I also thought about my friend Bud, who was teaching me about love. Uncle Martin closed that day with words that will forever echo in the annals of history. "Let Freedom ring . . . we will be able to speed up that day when all of God's children, black men and white men, Jews and Gentiles, Protestants and Catholics, will be able to join hands and sing in the words of the old Negro spiritual, "Free at last. Free at last. Thank God almighty, we are free at last!"

Then that nice old man, Benjamin Mays, brought the benediction.

Roy Wilkins, head of the NAACP; A. Philip Randolph, leader of the march; and Whitney Young, head of the Urban League.

Riverside Church in New York City prepared 80,000 box lunches for the participants in the March on Washington.

Halfway around the world, people in Tel Aviv, Israel, marched in support of the Civil Rights Bill.

In Geneva, Switzerland, Americans abroad lent their voices.

I Have a Dream . . .

Five score years ago, a great American, in whose symbolic shadow we stand today, signed the Emancipation Proclamation. This momentous decree came as a great beacon light of hope to millions of Negro slaves who had been seated in the flames of withering injustice. It came as a joyous daybreak to end the long night of their captivity.

But one hundred years later, the Negro still is not free. One hundred years later, the life of the Negro is still sadly crippled by the manacles of segregation and the chains of discrimination. One hundred years later, the Negro lives on a lonely island of poverty in the midst of a vast ocean of material prosperity. One hundred years later, the Negro is still languished in the corners of American society and finds himself an exile in his own land. So we've come here today to dramatize a shameful condition.

In a sense we've come to our nation's capital to cash a check. When the architects of our republic wrote the magnificent words of the Constitution and the Declaration of Independence, they were signing a promissory note to which every American was to fall heir. This note was a promise that all men—yes, black men as well as white men—would be guaranteed the unalienable rights of life, liberty, and the pursuit of happiness.

It is obvious today that America has defaulted on this promissory note insofar as her citizens of color are concerned. Instead of honoring this sacred obligation, America has given the Negro people a bad check; a check which has come back marked "insufficient funds." But we refuse to believe that the bank of justice is bankrupt. We refuse to believe that there are insufficient funds in the great vaults of opportunity of this nation. So we've come to cash this check—a check that will give us upon demand the riches of freedom and the security of justice. We have also come to this hallowed spot to remind America of the fierce urgency of now. This is no time to engage in the luxury of cooling off or to take the tranquilizing drug of gradualism. Now is the time to make real the promises of Democracy. Now is the time to rise from the dark and desolate valley of segregation to the sunlit path of racial justice. Now is the time to lift our nation from the quicksands of racial injustice to the solid rock of brotherhood.

Now is the time to make justice a reality for all of God's children.

It would be fatal for the nation to overlook the urgency of the moment. This sweltering summer of the Negro's legitimate discontent will not pass until there is an invigorating autumn of freedom and equality. Nineteen sixty-three is not an end, but a beginning. Those who hope that the Negro needed to blow off steam and will now be content, will have a rude awakening if the nation returns to business as usual. There will be neither rest nor tranquility in America until the Negro is granted his citizenship rights. The whirlwinds of revolt will continue to shake the foundations of our nation until the bright day of justice emerges.

There is something that I must say to my people who stand on the warm threshold which leads into the palace of justice. In the process of gaining our rightful place we must not be guilty of wrongful deeds. Let us not seek to satisfy our thirst for freedom by drinking from the cup of bitterness and hatred.

We must forever conduct our struggle on the high plane of dignity and discipline. We must not allow our creative protest to degenerate into physical violence. Again and again we must rise to the majestic heights of meeting physical force with soul force. The marvelous new militancy which has engulfed the Negro community must not lead us to a distrust of all while people, for many of our white brothers, as evidenced by their presence here today, has come to realize that their destiny is tied up with our destiny. They have come to realize their freedom is inextricably bound to our freedom. We cannot walk alone.

As we walk, we must make the pledge that we shall always march ahead. We cannot turn back. There are those who are asking the devotees of civil rights, "When will you be satisfied?" We can never be satisfied as long as the Negro is the victim of the unspeakable horrors of police brutality. We can never be satisfied as long as our bodies, heavy with the fatigue of travel, cannot gain lodging in the motels of the highways and the hotels of the cities. We cannot be satisfied as long as a Negro in Mississippi cannot vote and a Negro in New York believes he has nothing for which to vote. No, no we are not satisfied, and we will not be satisfied, until justice rolls down like water and righteousness like a mighty stream.

I am not unmindful that some of you have come here out of great trials and tribulations. Some of you have come fresh from narrow jail cells. Some of you have come from areas where your quest for freedom left you battered by the storms of persecution and staggered by the winds of police brutality. You have been the veterans of creative suffering. Continue to work with the faith that unearned suffering is redemptive.

Go back to Mississippi, go back to Alabama, go back to South Carolina, go back to Georgia, go back to Louisiana, go back to the slums and ghettos of our Northern cities, knowing that somehow this situation can and will be changed. Let us not wallow in the valley of despair.

I say to you today, my friends, though even though we face the difficulties of today and tomorrow, I still have a dream. It is a dream deeply rooted in the American dream.

I have a dream that one day this nation will rise up and live out the true meaning of its creed: "We hold these truths to be self-evident: that all men are created equal."

I have a dream that one day on the red hills of Georgia the sons of former slaves and the sons of former slave owners will be able to sit down together at the table of brotherhood.

I have a dream that one day even the state of Mississippi, a state sweltering with the heat of injustice, sweltering with the heat of oppression, will be transformed into an oasis of freedom and justice.

I have a dream that my four little children will one day live in a nation where they will not be judged by the color of their skin but by the content of their character.

I have a dream today.

I have a dream that one day down in Alabama, with its vicious racists, with its governor having his lips dripping with the words of interposition and nullification, one day right there in Alabama little black boys and black girls will be able to join hands with little white boys and white girls as sisters and brothers.

I have a dream today.

I have a dream that one day every valley shall be exalted, every hill and mountain shall be made low, the rough places will be made plain, and the crooked places will be made straight, and the glory of the Lord shall be revealed, and all flesh shall see it together.

This is our hope. This is the faith that I go back to the South with. With this faith we will be able to hew out of the mountain of despair a stone of hope. With this faith we will be able to transform the jangling discords of our nation into a beautiful symphony of brotherhood. With this faith we will be able to work together, to pray together, to struggle together, to go to jail together, to stand up for freedom together, knowing that we will be free one day.

This will be the day when all of God's children will be able to sing with new meaning, "My country 'tis of thee, sweet land of liberty, of thee I sing. Land where my fathers died, land of the pilgrim's pride, from every mountainside, let freedom ring."

And if America is to be a great nation this must become true. So let freedom ring from the prodigious hilltops of New Hampshire. Let freedom ring from the mighty mountains of New York. Let freedom ring from the heightening Alleghenies of Pennsylvania.

Let freedom ring from the snowcapped Rockies of Colorado!

Let freedom ring from the curvacious slopes of California!

But not only that; let freedom ring from Stone Mountain of Georgia!

Let freedom ring from Lookout Mountain of Tennessee. Let freedom ring from every hill and molehill of Mississippi. From every mountainside, let freedom ring.

And when this happens, when we allow freedom [to] ring, when we let it ring from every village and every hamlet, from every state and every city, we will be able to speed up that day when all of God's children, black men and white men, Jews and Gentiles, Protestants and Catholics, will be able to join hands and sing in the words of the old Negro spiritual, "Free at last! Free at last! Thank God almighty, we are free at last!"

—The Reverend Martin Luther King Jr.

Stars for freedom (from top): Unidentified, Frank Silvera, James Garner, Marlon Brando, Steve Cochran, Tony Franciosa, Rita Moreno, and Harry Belafonte.

(Top middle): Director Joseph Mankiewicz; Charlton Heston; author James Baldwin.

Placard-bearing demonstrators on Constitution Avenue.

(Top right) Opera singer Marian Anderson; Roy Wilkins of the NAACP; Paul Newman; Robert Spike of the National Council of Churches; actress Faye Emerson.

(Bottom left) Ralph addresses the crowd. (Bottom right) Comedian/activist Dick Gregory.

"The Negro baby born in America today, regardless of the section or the state in which he is born, has about one-half as much chance of completing high school as a white baby born in the same place, on the same day; one-third as much chance of completing college; one-third as much chance of becoming a professional man; twice as much chance of becoming unemployed; about one-seventh as much chance of earning $10,000 a year; a life expectancy which is seven years shorter, and the prospects of earning only half as much.

"The nation can properly be proud of the demonstration that has occurred here today."

—President John F. Kennedy

Birmingham
Sunday, September 15, 1963

After the March on Washington, euphoria hung in the air, yet there were angry rumblings among members of the KKK. At the annual children's day at 16th Street Baptist Church, the Sunday school lesson was "A Love That Forgives." Cynthia Wesley, in her little red sweater, and her adoptive father made breakfast for her ailing adopted mother, "Dear." Addie Mae and Sarah Collins, wearing dresses sewn by their mother, played as they walked to church with their older sisters. Denise McNair, daughter of a photographer, was sleepy that morning after staying up late with relatives. Carol Robertson and her brother were dropped off at Sunday school by their parents.

Just before Sunday school ended, the five little girls met in the sky-blue ladies' rest room. The morning light streamed through the basement window as they stood in an open area. A teacher came into the rest room, reminded the girls to hurry for the upcoming assembly, washed her hands, and left. Sarah, age 11, went into the end stall to use the facilities as the other girls straightened their dresses. In that instant, the rest room exploded. The explosion ripped apart the walls and the fragile bodies of Cynthia, Denise, Addie Mae, and Carol.

Pandemonium erupted. Pastor John Cross thought that everyone was all right as he walked through the empty Sunday school basement. The clock had stopped at 10:27. Then Mr. Lay, the civil defense worker, showed him the gaping hole in the side of the church. They entered cautiously, fearing another explosion, and dug through the rubble to find the four little bodies literally lying on top of one another. "They must have clung together," said Rev. Cross. As he and the defense workers were about to give up the search, a small, whimpering voice was heard from the corner of the room. Sarah had survived, but was blinded in one eye by the blast. Later that day, while riding his bicycle, 13-year-old Virgil Ware was shot and killed by two white youths after they attended a Klan rally.

"Come 'round by my side and I'll sing you a song, I'll sing it softly, it'll do no one harm. On Birmingham Sunday, the blood ran like wine, and the choir kept singing of freedom."

—Richard Farina

An hour into the service, Daddy stepped to the pulpit with tears in his eyes and asked that we bow our heads and humble our hearts in prayer for the innocent little girls who were killed that morning at the close of Sunday school. This was my first encounter with death. I was stricken with fear as we ran around the church waiting for Daddy. I froze in the narrow alleyway beside the church. I couldn't move for fear that a bomb might go off and I would be killed, too. My oldest brother ran back and kept reassuring me as he took my hand in his and led me through the dark alley. It was a quiet Sunday dinner that night, as we dined with the King family. That evening after I said my prayers for bed, the nightmare of the bombing began. It continued to recur for the next thirty years.

Cynthia Wesley
1949–1963

Addie Mae Collins
1949–1963

Denise McNair
1951–1963

Carol Robertson
1949–1963

There's a sweet, sweet spirit in this place
And I know that it's the spirit of the Lord

—Traditional Hymn

A mother...

A sister...

A family...

Last rites for Cynthia Wesley were given by Pastor John H. Cross as Ralph prayed.

FREEDOM SUMMER
Harvest of Hate

I know that black is beautiful and that white is beautiful. But the most beautiful color of all is black and white together.

We hate each other because we fear each other. We fear each other because we don't know each other. We don't know each other because we won't sit down at the table together.

—RDA

described as 'massive insistence' upon drastic changes in the American social structure to achieve the goal of total integration. They abandoned patience, rejected tokenism and gradualism. This mood pervaded the entire Negro community, as seen by the tremendous outpouring of thousands of Negroes into the streets of the nation. Blacks withstood police violence, kickings, beatings, the use of fierce dogs, firehoses, and murder. In 1963 alone, there were more than 930 public protest demonstrations in 115 cities, in 15 Southern and border states. More than 20,083 persons, Negro and white, who had participated in these demonstrations, were arrested. Thirty-five bombings took place and 10 people were killed as a result of racial strife. 1963 was marked by defiance of the federal government by the governor of Alabama; the bombing of 16th Street Baptist Church, killing four innocent little girls; the murder of Virgil Ware, another Negro child on the streets of Birmingham later that day; the fatal shooting in the back of NAACP official Medgar Evers; and the assassination of our beloved president, John Fitzgerald Kennedy. Clearly one could see that this was our most serious domestic crisis since the Civil War.

◇

The *Washington Star* editorial of June 2, 1963, described this as the 'second American Revolution. The current outbreak by Negroes . . . is a manifestation of a genuine and justified revolution as any of the revolutions in history; history being largely an account of a sequence of revolutions.' The mood for 'Freedom Now' pervades the entire Negro community and countless numbers of white friends. This fact was seen when a quarter of a million people marched on

the nation's capitol for jobs and freedom. The present revolution is an attempt to gain the rights guaranteed all citizens in the Declaration of Independence, the Constitution of the United States, and the Amendments of the Constitution. The first agenda is the passage of the Civil Rights Bill in its present form, which is now before the Senate. The bill must not be weakened—the filibuster broken—and the bill must be passed. The continued denial of these rights to some citizens by certain states solely because of their race brought us to this critical hour in the life of our nation and made 'race' one of the foremost problems of our time. The future of this nation will depend to a large degree upon the solution of the race problem. 'A house divided cannot stand against itself.' The nations of the world are saying to America today in no uncertain terms, 'We can not hear what you say about liberty and justice for all, for seeing how you practice inequality for some.' In spite of our wealth, our scientific and technological advancements, our might and power, unless we learn to respect the worth and dignity of all human persons, we shall be destroyed by wickedness, ignorance, and barbarity. Let us seek to redeem the soul of America and create a society built on love and brotherhood. For 'out of one blood, God created all nations to dwell upon the face of the earth,' says the Holy Bible. We are all brothers, made in the image and likeness of God which must lead us all to know that there is but one race and that is the human race. Remember, 'verily I say unto you, in as much as ye did it not to one of the least of these ye did it not to me?'

"The issues involved in this confrontation are moral as well as legal. The Negro is causing the nation to gain a new image of himself. For it is in our tradition that when people have self-respect, nothing can keep them from asserting the inalienable rights of free men, women, and children. I emphasize children, for in most instances children have led the crusade for human dignity. They left behind astonished teachers, troubled parents, school boards, city officials, and the police force. For their freedom, they marched all over Alabama, Mississippi, Georgia, South Carolina, Florida, Virginia, North Carolina, and Louisiana. Twenty million Negro Americans have reached the end of patience with America's slow pace of social change. But the concept of using nonviolent means to achieve justifiable ends did not originate with the American Negro. It is as old as Moses' struggle with the Egyptian pharaoh and embraces the same justifications—an outraged sense of justice and a constant reliance on God's leadership. Nonviolence is the only practical protest available to a minority. Our Movement is rooted in the philosophy of love as manifested by Thoreau, Mahatma Gandhi, and Christ. We will not turn to violence nor will we retaliate with violence. 'Put down thy sword, for he who fighteth with the sword will perish by the sword.' If the philosophy of 'an eye for an eye, and a tooth for a tooth' is followed to its ultimate conclusion then we will eventually end up with a blind and toothless society. And can the blind lead the blind? We must receive these ends through love in race relations—for love is the most powerful force known to man.

Upon my release from jail in Birmingham last summer after several weeks of confinement, I rushed to Atlanta to see my wife, my two daughters, and my son. After the kissing and hugging was over, my youngest daughter, Donzaleigh, just five years of age, looked at me and asked, 'Daddy, are you out of jail now?' I then assured her that this was so. She then said, 'Oh, I am so happy, we are now free?' I said to her, 'No my darling, we are not completely free yet.' My child then said, 'Well Daddy, you go back to jail and stay there until you win us freedom. I want to be free.' What could I say to my innocent child? Then I remembered Lincoln's words. 'Men will soon forget what we say here, but not what we do here.' Beyond a shadow of a doubt, the Movement in this country to gain total freedom for the Negro can accurately be called the most moving drama of the 20th century. Truth shall cover the earth, like the waters cover the sea. And if we accept the challenge of this age, 'men will beat their swords into plowshares, their spears into pruning hooks and study war no more.'"

—RDA
From the speech
"Accepting the Challenge of This Age:
Love and Race Relations."
The American Baptist Convention
May 19, 1964

Pittsburgh, Pennsylvania

On May 2, 1964, Methodists kneel in prayer during a vigil protesting the church's inadequate stand on integration.

"It is an old but true maxim that 11 o'clock on Sunday morning is the most segregated hour in America, and that Sunday school is the most segregated school of the week. Let there be religious equality and integration in our churches—the houses of God. Many Negroes have been arrested for attempting to attend religious services where the pastor and congregation are white. Also, white friends who have sought to worship in churches with Negroes were arrested or ridiculed. I call upon the churches to take a more active stand in supporting the Movement to build better race relations through love. Let the church be a voice rather than an echo; a light rather than a reflection."

—RDA, May 19, 1964

Tuscaloosa, Alabama

One of several hundred demonstrators hauled away in 1964.

Six hundred demonstrators caused a traffic jam as they tried to integrate restaurants.

The mothers of the slain civil rights workers: (from left) Mrs. Chaney, Mrs. Goodman, and Mrs. Schwerner.

Sgt. Wallace Miller, a witness to the murders who honorably informed the FBI.

Sheriff Lawrence Rainey (left) and Deputy Cecil Price (second from left), the alleged killers and organizers of the mob of eighteen men responsible for the murders. The officers were found not guilty.

Martin, Ralph, District of Columbia congressman Walter Fauntroy, and Andy Young met with FBI director J. Edgar Hoover to commend him on the FBI's efforts to find the three missing civil rights workers, even though Hoover had blatantly bugged their offices, hotels, cars, and homes for years. Hoover called Martin "the most notorious liar," and made considerable efforts to defame Martin's personal character in order to stop the Civil Rights Movement. History has revealed that J. Edgar Hoover, his supporters, and the recent exploiters of the unethical FBI wiretapping were adversaries of the ideology of civil rights.

The Civil Rights Bill was signed on July 2, 1964.

Back on the road, again.

THE ROAD TO SELMA
The Right to Vote

Stony the road we've trod, bitter the
      chastening rod,
Felt in the days when hope unborn had died;
Yet with a steady beat, have not our weary feet,
Come to the place for which our fathers sighed?
We have come over a way that with tears have
      been watered,
We have come, treading our path through the
      blood of the slaughtered;
Out from the gloomy past, 'til now we stand
      at last,
Where the white gleam, of our bright star
      is cast...
Facing the rising sun, of a new day begun,
Let us march on, 'til victory is won!

—"Lift Every Voice and Sing"

149

he road to Selma is laden with blood, sacrifice, and tears. Down Highway 80 lies the route from Selma to Montgomery. It is on this dusty, turbulent country highway that many people have lost their lives, due to malicious acts of hatred and violence. But it was also here that black people won the right to vote.

The Civil Rights Act of 1964 became law that July and with it, racial barriers to Negroes voting in the deep South were destroyed. The law specified that voter registration standards must be the same for everyone, literacy was based upon a minimum of a sixth grade education, and prospective voters could not be disqualified because of minor errors on their registration applications. However, due to stalling tactics and continued discrimination by local officials, blacks were still not allowed to vote in the 'black belts' of Alabama, Mississippi, and Louisiana. New direct legislation was needed to address the issues of voting so that Southern officials would have to comply with the laws.

The year was 1965 and we had been trying to decide whether or not we could force the federal government to act on the persistent denial of voting rights to blacks in the South. We wanted a voting rights bill passed by Congress, and we knew that we would never get one unless the American people saw what was going on in places like Selma and registered enough indignation to force elected representatives into action.

In many ways the right to vote was the one right that ensured all other rights. Obviously, the federal government could not patrol every bus line and every restaurant throughout the South. If public transportation and public accommodations were to remain equally accessible to blacks—and that was now the law—then local authorities would have to share equal responsibility for seeing that their states and communities created a climate in which the law was obeyed.

"Selma served as an ideal illustration of what we had to face throughout the South. After Congress had passed the 1964 Civil Rights Bill, blacks in Selma had begun to pressure local authorities and businessmen to comply with federal statutes. But when black organizations such as the Dallas County Voters League began to meet to discuss ways of bringing about compliance, a state judge, James Hare, issued an injunction forbidding all public gatherings. Judge Hare's injunction stood for months and its very presence in Alabama was reason enough for us to go to Selma. Hare was quoted in the *New York Times* as saying 'Your Negro is a mixture of African types like the Congolite who has a long heel and the blue-gummed Ebo whose I.Q. is about 50 or 55.'

"In May 1964, we met at the Gaston Motel in Birmingham to talk about strategy in general and Selma in particular. Mrs. Amelia Boynton of the Dallas County Voters League was present and told us of the difficulties they had encountered, and of the devastating effect Judge Hare's injunction had on activists in and around Selma who wanted to press for voter registration. She pointed out that if this injunction were allowed to stand, then not only would we be unable to push for new civil rights legislation, but we would be unable to seek enforcement of those laws already passed. We would have won a great battle only to lose the war. She pleaded for us to come to Selma.

"I was convinced that we needed to look no further for a site to fight our next battle. We should choose Selma and

MARTIN LUTHER KING AT COMMUNIST TRAINING SCHOOL

challenge Judge Hare's injunction. Blacks were no allowed to vote and nothing would change the climate o southern states as much as the emergence of a strong black electorate, one that could mean the difference ir a close race between a racial extremist and a racial moderate. We merely wanted to get the vote in order to make a difference, to exercise our right as citizens, to choose who would govern us—whether black or white We wanted equal protection under the law—the right to enjoy the full privileges of American citizenship. We knew we could not elect blacks to office—yet. But we believed that we could use our voting strength through- out the region to elect people sympathetic to blacks anc protective of our rights.

"January 1, I was chosen to make the opening appearance Just before I left for Selma, Martin gave me some words o advice. 'Go down there, speak, get in your car, and drive right on back.' I detected an ominous note in his voice 'Do you have reason to believe there might be danger?' I asked him. 'There's been some evidence to that effect. 'What evidence?' I asked. 'There was an incident involving a snake,' he said. 'Somebody put a rattlesnake in the mail box of one of our supporters. Fortunately he heard some thing moving inside the box when he tried to pick up hi mail. It was a live snake and it could have killed him. When I got to Selma I found the crowd was extremely enthusiastic. Following Martin's advice, I didn't linger too long, but got back into the car and headed toward Mont- gomery, scanning the rearview mirror all the way. No one followed me.

"January 2, the SCLC [Southern Christian Leadership Con- ference] staff of Reverends C. T. Vivian, James Bevel Bernard Lafayette, and Andrew Young moved into Lowndes County near Selma to rally locals to register to vote.

"Selma would prove to be the most significant accomplish- ment of the Civil Rights Movement. Without the right to vote and the power to exercise that right, southerr Negroes would be defenseless."

—RD

(Right) The Lowndes County registrar threatened Martin and Ralph as they tried to seek his cooperation in registering voters.

As I stood beside my father's hospital bed, weeks before he died, he told me about Colonel Lingo, the violent chief of the Alabama state troopers, and his compatriot, Sheriff Jim Clark of Dallas County. He had had a personal violent encounter with Lingo, which finally gave me understanding to the years of his silent trepidation when we drove down Highway 80 to visit relatives in the country, and why after one encounter we could not stop for food or use the public facilities along this route from Montgomery to Selma.

(Left) Sheriff Jim Clark ordered Ralph and Martin to "get off of the sidewalk" as Negroes lined up to register to vote. At a mass meeting, Ralph later nominated Clark as an honorary member of the Negro Dallas County Voters League because of all the national media generated from his assault on Amelia Boynton. By February 7, "worn out" according to his aides, Sheriff Clark was hospitalized. On February 16, in front of television cameras, Sheriff Clark struck the Rev. C. T. Vivian on the steps of the Dallas County Courthouse. Witnesses reported that the sheriff, who weighed about 220 pounds, punched the tall, thin Vivian in the mouth after Vivian, calling him "brutal" and "like Hitler," dared the sheriff to hit him. Vivian was then arrested and charged with criminal provocation and contempt of court. Clark later claimed that he didn't remember hitting Vivian. "One of the first things I ever learned was not to hit a nigger with your fist because his head is too hard—of course, the camera might make me a liar."

Voting in Alabama in 1965

	Black Residents	Registered Black Voters	White Residents	Registered White Voters
Dallas County	32,687	320	23,952	9,463
Lowndes County	12,439	0	2,978	2,250
Marengo County	16,834	295	10,264	6,280
Perry County	11,415	289	5,943	3,006
Wilcox County	14,598	0	4,143	2,974
	87,973	904	47,280	23,973

With the majority of the black population being denied the right to vote in the Deep South, the white segregationists controlled the ballot boxes and subsequently the power structure of Alabama. It had been said that in the South, black people were recognized but their rights as individuals were ignored. (In the North, however, black people were ignored, but their legal rights were recognized.) Alabama governor George Wallace made excuses, saying that state officials were not involved with the voting rights issue in Selma, because it was a "local matter." However, he had been assured that there were times when the Voter Registration Office was open and no black people came in to register to vote. Wallace said, "There has been ample time to register anybody qualified under the state law." The voter-registration test proved to be so difficult that even some federal judges flunked it. Alabama state officials said that the test was difficult only for black people who couldn't read or write. They believed that blacks didn't want to read or write because the system had "given them so many opportunities" and they had "failed to appreciate or take advantage of them, therefore they shouldn't be allowed to vote." Governor Wallace had even complained that the voter-registration test should be "stiffer to protect the ballot."

After Ralph prayed, Martin surveyed the crowd.

During a night march on February 18—following a Sunday prayer meeting—Jimmie Lee Jackson was shot twice in the stomach, clubbed in the head, and killed. Jimmie Lee, a quiet, 26-year-old native of Perry County—a $6-a-day pulpwood worker and the youngest deacon of the rural St. James Baptist Church—told hospital officials before he died on February 26 that an Alabama state trooper had shot him. He had tried five times since turning 21 to register to vote.

Jimmie Lee's 82-year-old grandfather, Cagen Lee, recalled that he was behind the church when white men in helmets came running through the alley, knocking him down. One of the officers said, "Goddamn, this is old Cagen . . . don't hit him anymore," so Cagen knew they must have been local boys. His head bleeding, Cagen went to get Jimmie, who was in the café with his mother,

Viola. The troopers stormed the cafe, ordered everyone to leave, and began flailing Jimmie and Viola. Viola said, "The troopers had Jimmie Lee down on the floor, beating him"—and then they started beating her. Jimmie, bent over in pain, ran outside, followed by four or five troopers who continued to beat him as he tried to get away. No one in his family saw him get shot. When the assault was over, Viola would need four stitches in her head, Jimmie Lee would lie dying in the hospital, and a broken nightstick was all that remained on the streets of Marion.

Martin, in his eulogy for Jimmie Lee Jackson, said, "His death says we must all work passionately and unrelentingly . . . it is going to make us more determined now. We are going to march in the streets of Alabama until every Negro can vote."

The Second Attempt to Cross the Edmund Pettus Bridge

In greater numbers and with more organization, Martin, Ralph, and hundreds of followers attempted a second crossing of the Edmund Pettus Bridge to begin the 54-mile walk to Montgomery. They were carried by a jubilant spirit of impending victory despite daily death threats. When the road was blocked, they could walk no farther. Ralph prayed and Martin turned the crowd around. Years later, Martin and Ralph would joke that they prayed with their eyes open in case of an another bloody assault.

Montgomery, Alabama

On March 16, 1965, black and white college students from around the country converged on Montgomery in a massive sit-in demanding "one man, one vote" for everyone equally. Again the Alabama authorities responded with violent assaults.

Ralph, James Forman of SNCC, Martin, S. L. Douglas, John Lewis, and C. K. Steele march in the rain to the Montgomery Courthouse carrying the endorsement and flags of the United Nations for the right to vote and the right to march from Selma to Montgomery.

The Selma to Montgomery March

The 54-mile crusade for the right to vote began on March 21, 1965, at Brown's Chapel in Selma and ended on March 25 on the steps of the Alabama capitol in Montgomery. Thousands marched under the protection of the U.S. Army, which had been sent to Selma by President Johnson to uphold justice. Marchers walked through Lowndes County, home to 12,000 Negro residents. In the "black belt," rural Negroes outnumbered whites three to one, yet hardly any could vote. For the few that could, threats by the KKK kept them away from the polls.

At the rally before the march, Ralph told the crowd, "When we get to Montgomery we are going to go up to Governor Wallace's door and say, 'George, it's all over now. We've got the ballot!'" Then Martin said, "You will be the people that will write a new chapter in the history of our nation. Those of us who are Negroes don't have much. We have known the long night of poverty. Because of the system, we don't have much education, and some of us don't know how to make our nouns and verbs agree. But

thank God we have our bodies, our feet, and our souls. Walk together, children, and don't you get weary, and it will lead us to the promised land." With those words, they began the third and final march across the Edmund Pettus Bridge.

Martin and Ralph were joined by Ralph Bunche, Nobel laureate and undersecretary to the United Nations; Gary Merrill, actor and husband of film star Bette Davis; Dick Gregory; Jim Letherer, a physically challenged man with one leg who walked the 54 miles to Montgomery; a united coalition of clergy and nuns; and a host of other political and social figures. They wore leis of peace brought by the Hawaiian delegation.

John Lewis, Ralph, and Martin.

Martin and Coretta.

Martin, Coretta, and Ralph.

Ralph, Juanita, and Martin.

Harry Belafonte, Anthony Perkins, and Martin.

Martin, Coretta, Donzaleigh,
Ralph III, and Juandalynn.

Peter, Paul and Mary.

Juandalynn embraces Sammy Davis Jr. Donzaleigh (in Ralph's lap) awaits her kiss. Ralph Bunche is in the background.

Gary Merrill and Jim Letherer.

Everyone was extremely grateful to Harry Belafonte for all the money he helped to raise over the years and all the artists he invited to join the struggle for freedom, including Tony Bennett, Lena Horne, Diahann Carroll, Tony Perkins, Paul Newman, Eartha Kitt, Bobby Darin, James Baldwin, and more. But it was the passionate involvement of Marlon Brando and Sidney Poitier that taught me the underlying commitment to excellence in art and politics.

Juandalynn, Ralph III, and Donzaleigh lead John Lewis, Ralph, Juanita, and the marchers.

Left foreground: Bernard Lee; front row, left to right: A. Philip Randolph, John Lewis, Ralph, Juanita, Ralph Bunche, Ralph III, Martin, and Coretta. To the right: Yolanda Williams is being carried by Hosea.

It had begun to rain as we stood on the front line at St. Jude's Hospital on the morning of the march. Mother made us put on those plastic accordion rain caps. I wanted to hold my sister's hand, but Daddy wanted Ralph III in the middle, so I was forced to hold my brother's hand. I wanted to cry, but I had too much pride, because the cameras kept flashing as we waited for this monumental march to begin. I felt special that day, because I was doing my part for humanity. We, the children, alone were the front line. Daddy led the march until Martin and Aunt Coretta arrived. Some of the spectators yelled vile words and made threats. As a precaution, the children were moved to the second row. The National Guard had come to protect us, since there had been violence in Selma. But I felt safe that day in Montgomery. When my father stood up to speak, the crowd roared and cheered before he even said a word. I don't remember what he said. I was still too little, yet willing to serve.

171

"It was a glorious homecoming for Martin and me. Juanita and Coretta joined us in our moment of triumph, and we stood before our friends as they cheered our triumph over the Alabama white establishment. I made sure that our children, Juandalynn, Donzaleigh, and Ralph III—all of whom were born in Montgomery—were among the marchers. In fact, they led us up to Dexter Avenue.... They too were freedom fighters. We came from Selma to Montgomery—a distance of more than 50 miles. We had come from the outer regions of second-class citizenship to the threshold of full participation in American democracy. Everybody understood that our march had been more than a symbolic journey. For that hour we owned the capitol of the state of Alabama, just as for four days we had owned Highway 80.

"In Martin's speech, he said, 'They told us we wouldn't get here, and there were those who said we would get here only over their dead bodies, but all the world today knows that we are here and that we are standing before the forces of power in the state of Alabama saying, "We ain' goin' to let nobody turn us around."

I know you are asking today, "How long will it take?" I come to say to you this afternoon, however difficult the moment, however frustrating the hour, it will not be long, because truth pressed to earth will rise again. How long? Not long, because no lie can live forever. How long? Not long, because you still reap what you sow. How long? Not long, because the arm of the moral universe is long but it bends toward justice. How long? Not long, 'cause mine eyes have seen the glory of the coming of the Lord.... His truth is marching on. He has sounded forth the trumpets that shall never call retreat. He is lifting up the hearts of man before His judgment seat. Oh, be swift, my soul, to answer Him. Be jubilant, my feet. Our God is marching on.'

"The crowd roared its approval, and 75 yards away, in a window of his office, George Wallace parted the venetian blinds and peered out at twenty-five thousand people gathered for justice on the square."

—RDA

James J. Reeb

The Rev. James J. Reeb, a 38-year-old white Unitarian minister from Boston, Massachusetts, who joined a pilgrimage of 2,000 clergymen and nuns going to the South, was beaten by five Selma whites after he dined in a local black restaurant. Rev. Reeb died on March 11 of skull fractures. Greek Orthodox archbishop Iakovos; Dr. Dana Greely, president of the Unitarian Universal Association; Walter Reuther of the United Auto Workers; Martin; Ralph; and Andrew Young carried a single wreath—contributed by the American Friends Service Committee of Bucks County, Pennsylvania—to the Dallas County Courthouse in honor of Rev. Reeb.

This violence outraged the nation, prompting Congress to pass the Voting Rights Act, signed into law on August 6, 1965. The U.S. Commission on Civil Rights through the Justice Department, along with the essential extensions of the Voting Rights Act, helped to protect against voting discrimination and prevent implementation of gerrymandering and election manipulation techniques. The Voting Rights Act not only secured the right to vote for disenfranchised black Americans, but enforced legal voting practices and opened opportunities for Native and Latino Americans.

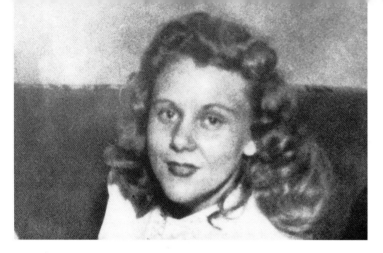

Viola Liuzzo

On the evening following the close of the Selma to Montgomery March, Viola Gregg Liuzzo, a Grand Rapids, Michigan, housewife and mother of five, and an honorable woman of conscience, appalled by what she saw on the news about the racial injustices in the South, was volunteering in Selma. Viola volunteered by driving black people to and from the Dallas County Courthouse to register to vote. On March 25th, during the last drive of a long day, Leroy Moton, a young 20-year-old black man, was her passenger.

That evening, Collie Leroy Wilkins, 21, Eugene Thomas, 42, William Orville Eaton, 41, and FBI informant Gary Thomas Rowe, 34, all white, went cruising around the city. Thomas was driving and Eaton sat next to him in the front of the automobile. Rowe and Wilkins sat in the rear. After about half an hour, the men pulled up to a traffic light. To their left was the automobile of Viola Liuzzo. They were astonished to see in the car "a white lady and a colored man." Eugene Thomas said, "Let's get 'em." The red light changed to green, Viola drove away, and the four men followed in their automobile.

All of the men had been sworn into the local chapter of the Ku Klux Klan, with a vow of silence to never betray the acts of Klan members. Thomas reached over and got his revolver from between the seats and announced, "Get your pistols, cousins." Wilkins took his pistol out.

At some points the cars reached speeds of 100 mph on Highway 80. Rowe tried to get Thomas to turn back. Thomas replied, "I done told you, Baby Brother, you're in the big time now. We're gonna take that automobile." Thomas then gave his pistol to Wilkins. In Viola's Northern hometown Viola's husband and five children awaited her return. Rowe recalled, "As we got almost even, Wilkins said 'Give it some gas.' Gene [Thomas] sped up a little bit and put our auto immediately beside the driver.... And just as we got even with the front window, the lady driving the automobile ... turned and looked around, directly facing the automobile. Thomas says, 'All right men, shoot the hell out of it.' Everybody started shooting. Wilkins and Eaton both emptied their revolvers toward the automobile." Rowe said that he only pretended to shoot.

The men shot Viola Liuzzo in her face and head. Her blood splattered all over Leroy Moton. With Viola's body slumped over the steering wheel, the car coasted off the road to a stop. Moton turned off the ignition and the lights. About five minutes later the car of killers came back to make sure that Viola and Moton were dead. The killers saw Viola's blood on Moton and the interior of the car covered in her blood and assumed that both passengers were dead. Satisfied, the men drove away.

Murder charges were brought against Collie Leroy Wilkins, Eugene Thomas, and William Orville Eaton based on the eyewitness testimony of Gary Rowe. The counsel for the defense in the Wilkins's trial turned the case into Southern courtroom drama. In his summation, the self-described "Imperial Klonsel" of the Ku Klux Klan called Mrs. Liuzzo "a white nigger," because in her personal effects was her membership card to the NAACP. The Klan defense counsel called Rowe—for breaking his oath to the KKK—a "liar, perjurer ... and worse than a white nigger!" The Klan lawyer said, "I'm proud I stand for white supremacy. Not black supremacy, not the mixing and mongrelizing of the races ... One white woman and these niggers.... Right there. Riding through your country.... 'We will overcome ...' what in God's name were they tryin' to overcome? To overcome God himself? And do unto white people what God said you shall not do because there'll be thorns in your eyes, thorns in your flesh. If you intermarry with a servile race, then you shall be destroyed!"

After ten hours of deliberation, the jury of twelve white men told Circuit Judge Werth Thagard that they were hopelessly deadlocked—eight voting to convict Wilkins of manslaughter, seven voting to acquit him. The judge sent them back and they returned deadlocked again, now with two in favor of acquittal. The two jurors both acknowledged their membership with the White Citizens Council, a white-collar version of the Klan. The judge declared a mistrial and sent the men home.

The Signing of the Voting Rights Act

"In our system, the first right and most vital of all our rights is the right to vote. Jefferson described the elective franchise as the 'arc of our safety.' It is from the exercise of this right that the guarantee of all our other rights flow.

"Unless the right to vote is secured and not denied, all other rights are insecure and subject to denial for all our citizens. The challenge of this right is a challenge as decisively as we would meet a challenge mounted against our land from enemies abroad.

"The harsh fact is that in many places in this country, men and women are kept from voting because they are Negroes. Every device has been used to deny this right.... The only way to pass these barriers is to show a white skin. This bill will strike down restrictions to voting in all elections—federal, state, and local—which have been used to deny Negroes the right to vote. Their cause must be our cause too. It is not just Negroes, but all of us, who must overcome the crippling legacy of bigotry...and We Shall Overcome."

—President Lyndon Baines Johnson

MISSISSIPPI TO MEMPHIS
Death of a Dreamer

Precious Lord, take my hand.

Lead me on, let me stand.

I am tired. I am weak. I am worn.

Through the storms, through the night,

Lead me on to the light.

Take my hand precious Lord

And lead me on.

—Thomas A. Dorsey
A Hymn

The years following Selma moved more slowly and were less dramatic. For the first time, we got the chance to really know and appreciate our fathers as fathers because they were home more often.

As we had been raised during the nonviolent Civil Rights Movement, Juanita thought it was time for the children to make their contribution. That fall, Juandalynn, Yolanda, Martin, Ralph III, and I integrated the first elementary school in Atlanta. It was a little bewildering for me to have the media present as I began elementary school, let alone to have a boy in my class call me "nigger" and another threaten to push my sister down the steps. But it was equally pleasant to have another boy offer to carry my books and demand that his friends treat me fairly.

After so much struggle and hard-ship, changes were finally being brought forth. With the passage of the Voting Rights Act, huge numbers of Negroes filled the polls of Birmingham, Alabama, for the first time since Reconstruction to vote in the Democratic primary. They nominated attorney Fred Gray to the Alabama State Legislature. The Voting Rights Act of 1965 would later require amendments by the Subcommittee of Civil and Constitutional Rights. It was and still is imperative that the United States Department of Justice be fully involved in the enforcement of the Voting Rights Act until the temporary and special provisions contained in the act—aimed at removing unconstitutional barriers to voting—are made permanent. On May 7, 1981, Ralph would testify before the United States Houes of Representatives for the extension of the special provisions. The Citizenship School, which began in 1961, was in full swing under the direction of Mrs. Dorothy Cotton and Mrs. Septima Clark. At the Dorchester Center, they taught leadership training to Southern rural black adults, who would then teach reading and writing to

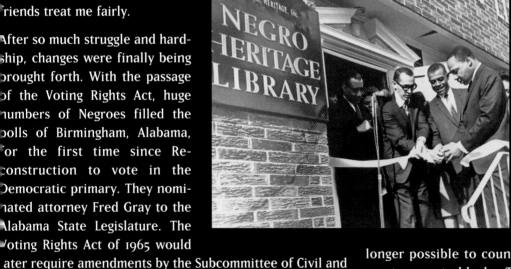

the uneducated so that they could pass the literacy test required to vote. The program gave all-around training in consumer education and community development such as housing, health, filing income tax forms, assistance to handicapped children, social security, and how the U.S. government operates. The Citizenship School improved the lives of blacks and provided fundamental information on citizenship that was unavailable through any other private or public program. The program was sponsored by the Southern Christian Leadership Conference through a grant from the Field Foundation. In 1967, 500 community leaders received teacher training at the Dorchester Center so that they could instruct the disenfranchised in their communities. Miss Mew Soong-Li helped pioneer an outstanding poverty program operated by local residents of Lowndes and Wilcox Counties. Before the Voting Rights Act of 1965, there were no black voters in these counties.

In Martin's address to the SCLC convention of 1967, he said that in 10 years, the Negro had caused "the sagging walls of segregation to come tumbling down." It was no longer possible to count the number of public establishments open to blacks. The Negro, who had seemed invisible and whose cause had been unknown to the majority of the nation, had dominated the pages of the press in the call for social justice.

The courage with which blacks confronted opponents, enraged mobs and dissolved the false, negative stereotypes perpetuated by the entertainment industry of the "black Mammie" and the grinning, submissive "Uncle Tom." However, years later the entertainment industry created negative, false images of the black lifestyle. In the nineteenth century, black dance, gestures, and stance were staples of entertainment in popular white American minstrels. During the 1830s, Thomas D. Rice became famous for his blackface minstrel routine, "Jim Crow." It was a "coon dance"—he would perform the grossly caricatured "idiosyncrasies" of black movement and style. This humor was founded on the exaggerated, supposed stupidity of the Negro. A blackfaced performer would prance around on stage, stumbling over his feet, then break into a story. Thomas Rice said that he based his routine on a song and dance he saw performed by a crippled elderly black man.

Martin said that the black man "came out of his struggle integrated only slightly in the external society, but powerfully integrated within. This was a victory that had to precede all other gains." Black people had to rise above these crippling images that inhibited the self-respect of generations of young people. Martin went on to say that "the Negro decided to straighten his back up, realizing that a man cannot ride your back unless it is bent."

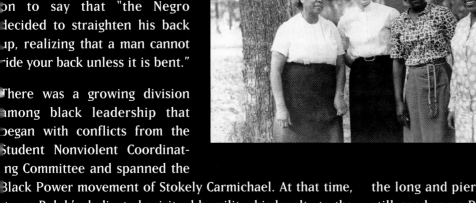

There was a growing division among black leadership that began with conflicts from the Student Nonviolent Coordinating Committee and spanned the Black Power movement of Stokely Carmichael. At that time, it was Ralph's dedicated spiritual humility, his loyalty to the mission of nonviolence, his unrelenting love for Martin, and his gentle, inspiring, faithful composure that calmed the warring factions of the Civil Rights Movement around Martin. Many young people began to lose faith in nonviolence. Despite its obvious successes, it fell prey to the pitfalls of fleeting media attention, self-promotion, and vanity. Militancy was rising, along with the appeal for violence in an effort to intimidate, resulting in the outbreak of riots. It was the painfully sad common man who would suffer the devas-

tation of the loss of his neighborhood. The indifferent white society watched the self-destruction of black neighborhoods from afar.

Despite their legislative achievements, blacks still lived at the bottom of the economic scale of American society. Although the doors had been forced partially open—a select few had advanced to higher levels—the majority of blacks still had their "mobility for advancement restricted." Martin said, "Negroes are still impoverished aliens in an affluent society. They are too poor to even rise with the society, too impoverished by the ages to be able to ascend by using their own resources." America, which was built by black labor, became the richest, most powerful nation, leaving the Negro behind while embracing new white emigrants to share in her wealth. Martin said America's tendency to ignore the Negro's inventions and contributions to American life, to "strip him of his personhood, is as old as the earliest history books and as contemporary as the morning's newspaper." Martin declared that we had "crossed the Red Sea that for years had been hardened by the long and piercing winter of passive resistance . . . we still need some Paul Reveres of conscience. . . . We need a chart, we need a compass. Indeed, we need some North Star to guide us into the future." Moreover, he asked, "Where do we go from here? First we must honestly recognize where we are now. To upset this cultural homicide, the Negro must rise up with an affirmation of his own Olympian manhood. As long as the mind is enslaved, the body can never be free. Psychological freedom, a firm sense of self esteem, is the most powerful weapon against the long night of physical slavery."

(Top) Black people in Birmingham line up at the polling booths for the first time in over a century. They successfully nominated Fred Gray in the Democratic primary.

(Bottom) Ralph, Juanita, James Forman, Coretta, Martin, and Sam Williams lead a march of 800 through downtown Atlanta to the Georgia State Capitol to protest "good ol' boy" politics and the ousting of State Representative–elect Julian Bond by the Georgia General Assembly. Despite the obvious intelligence and fortitude of black elected officials, it would be hard to soften the hearts of the Southern white officials who opposed the Civil Rights Bill and the Voting Rights Act. Years later, some of these opponents of justice would still be elected governor of Georgia.

(Opposite) The needs and rights of children were always of paramount importance to Martin and Ralph. Joan Baez (upper left), a faithful activist, joined Martin, Ralph, Hosea Williams, and Andrew Young on their pilgrimage to "feed the children." After Martin's death, Ralph was successful in getting the government to institute a free breakfast and lunch program for low income children.

Robert Francis Kennedy

Concerned about the poverty that was engulfing the South, and upon the advice of Marian Wright Edelman, Sen. Robert Kennedy traveled to Mississippi to see how the masses of poor black and white people were living in the rural South. He found great devastation and hunger, then returned to Washington with a renewed commitment to helping humanity, resolve the problems of poverty, and to run for president of the United States.

"Some men see things as they are and say, 'Why?' I dream things that never were and ask, 'Why not?'"

—Robert Francis Kennedy

MISSISSIPPI

The Southern Christian Leadership Conference (SCLC) convention in Jackson, Mississippi, was keynoted by Sen. Edward Kennedy (second from right), then among the youngest men in the U.S. Senate. The younger brother of John F. Kennedy made a rousing speech that Ralph said reminded many of the late president.

Hosea Williams (in foreground), James Forman, Martin, Ralph, and James Farmer of the Congress of Racial Equality (CORE), along with many others, crowd together in one of many hotel rooms to mull over solutions to the various problems they faced.

The Meredith March

James Meredith, who integrated the University of Mississippi, was shot on June 6, 1966, in Hernando, Mississippi, as he marched alone to encourage blacks to vote during the elections. His movement, "The March Against Fear," became known as the Meredith March, as civil rights leaders converged on Mississippi to take up his cross and finish his 16-day, 220-mile march. Meredith recovered from his wound and joined the march on June 26 near the end of the journey. Although I remember little about the march—just my walking with the handicapped Jim Letherer—my mother told me of her encounter with the cruel state troopers who made it difficult for her to leave the march and take us to the rest room. Sammy Davis Jr., Marlon Brando, Tony Franciosa, and Olympian Rafer Johnson joined the

Meredith March to lend their support. I suppose that is why Brando was always an influential figure in my life and one of the reasons why I would honor my grandmother's heritage and ask my father and Rev. John Adams to make arrangements for me to live among the Ogalala Sioux Indians on the Pine Ridge Reservation. I still remember my anxiety about returning to Mississippi years later as a teenager for SCLC's convention and seeing a KKK cross burning on the lawn of our Biloxi hotel as I stood on the balcony with Jesse, wondering when racism would end.

(Above) Leon Hall, Whitney Young, Juanita, Ralph, Coretta, Martin, and and Floyd McKissick lead the Meredith March.

Floyd McKissick, national director of CORE, Ralph David Abernathy, and Dick Gregory addressing reporters at the March Against Fear in Grenada, Mississippi, 1966.

Dr. Benjamin Spock joins Martin and Bernard Lee.

"The time has come for those of us who feel that this war is immoral and unjust to advise young men of the alternate to the draft, to serve as conscientious objectors . . . thousands and thousands of people, both adults and children, are being maimed and mutilated and killed in this war . . . I still feel and live by the principle, 'Thou shalt not kill.' And it is out of this moral commitment to dignity and the worth of human personality that I feel it is necessary to stand up against the war in Vietnam . . . we are committing atrocities equal to any perpetrated by the Vietcong. We are left standing before the world glutted by our own barbarity. We are engaged in a war that seeks to turn the clock of history back and perpetuate white colonialism . . . if America's soul becomes totally poisoned, part of the autopsy must read, 'Vietnam.' . . . We should admit to the world that we made a tragic mistake in Vietnam."

—MLK

In March of 1968 the garbage workers' strike began to occupy our attention. This strike came at a time when the economic plight of poor people was a major concern to Martin. He made one speech there late in March and was impressed by the response and fervor of the crowd. So he agreed to return and lead a nonviolent march. When the time came, he was in Newark, so I went ahead and delivered one of my best speeches in his absence. The next day our driver, Rev. Solomon Jones, took me to pick up Martin and Bernard Lee at the airport.

The waiting marchers at the AME church were growing impatient. Upon our arrival, we had planned to workshop the crowd in the techniques of nonviolence, but our vehicle was surrounded by a group of young men who wouldn't let us out of the car. Finally our host, Rev. James Lawson, the Memphis leader, pushed his way to us and suggested that the only way to gain control was to start the march. So we did. Then, after a few blocks, we heard what sounded like gunshots, though it was the smashing of glass windows. Invaders had used the cover of our march to commit acts of violence. Suddenly what had started out as a peaceful demonstration was turning into a riot, betraying our principles to lash out at the white community. There were shouts and screams. We heard whistles blow and then, in the distance, the whine of sirens. Looking behind, we could see people scattering in all directions.

Martin turned to Jim Lawson, the official leader, who was just ahead of us. 'Jim,' he yelled. 'There's violence breaking out, and I can't lead a violent march. Call it off!' Lawson shouted, 'The march is off! Everybody go home! The march is off!' 'Let's get out of here!' Martin shouted, but that was easier said than done.

We looked ahead and saw a chain of state troopers beginning to form. For an instant it looked like we would all be crowded in together, in a closing net. At a corner we saw a car, driven by a black woman, and suddenly a policeman stepped in behind her, indicating that her car would be the last allowed across the intersection. 'Let's get in that car,' Bernard said. 'They're letting her drive on.' The three of us pushed our way up to the car. The woman recognized us, and motioned for us to get in. Just then the state troopers began to lower their gas masks. They let us zoom across the intersection, and as we looked out the rear window we saw the canisters of tear gas flying through the air. In complete silence we drove till we reached the Mississippi River. We stayed that night at the Riverfront Holiday Inn—a two-bedroom suite with a living area in between. Bernard and I took the room with two beds, and Martin took the one with the single bed. He sat down immediately and turned on the television, and I realized how upset he was. We were getting live coverage of the riot. Martin shook his head in disbelief. 'This is terrible ... now we'll never get anybody to believe in nonviolence.' 'It's not our fault,' I told him. 'Those young men, the Invaders ...' 'It doesn't matter who did it ... we'll get the blame,' he said.

"That was the beginning of a long night. The television reported that the Invaders responsible for the riot had one of their group killed that morning and that they had been marching with Dr. King. The commentators made that point over and over. 'Never have I led a march where the demonstrators committed acts of violence,' Martin said. 'We should have workshopped the people,' he said. Then he brooded for hours. 'Maybe we'll just have to let violence have its chance,' he said. 'Maybe the people will listen to the voice of violence. They certainly won't listen to us.' But I disagreed. 'You know violence will never get us anywhere. We can't let these people take over. They'll ruin everything we've built up.' I pleaded with him to stop worrying and get some rest. Finally, about 4 A.M., he fell asleep and I tiptoed out, exhausted. It seemed as if I had just fallen asleep when I heard a bell ringing

When I opened the door I saw three young men standing here. 'We want to apologize for yesterday,' one said. 'Who are you?' 'We're the Invaders.' As a precaution, I looked over them carefully. They were well dressed, well groomed; and I didn't see any signs of weapons, so I let them in. They told me they had been wrong and that one of their friends had been killed during the skirmishes. They were deeply sorry. I listened, and then explained to them the reasons why nonviolence was the only way to freedom for black people. They said they understood and assured me that they were with us 100 percent. As I spoke with the Invaders, Martin prepared for the press conference. After they left, we dressed and dashed downstairs to strong interrogations by hostile newsmen.

Martin told the press precisely what had happened the day before. He was detailed and witty as he answered all the questions that were thrown at him in a firm, upbeat manner. It was perhaps his finest performance with the press.

'Martin,' I said, 'you were just great.' He smiled. 'Were you really pleased, Ralph?' he said. 'Completely pleased.' 'If you were pleased,' he said, 'then you can do something to please me.' 'What's that?' I asked. 'Get me out of Memphis!'

That night [back in Atlanta], Martin and Corrie, as he called her, came for dinner and brought fish for Juanita to fry. The Kings brought enough fish to feed three families, but as soon as Martin saw that Juanita had already cooked, he grabbed a bowl and took it into the family room. 'We'll eat some of this while the two of you fry fish.' He didn't talk about the Movement that night. Instead he talked about the times before the Montgomery bus boycott when we were all younger and hadn't taken on the burdens of black people. He remembered people long forgotten, did some of his comical imitations, and told stories. Juanita and Coretta brought in the platter of

fish . . . b) the time we finished, we were absolutely stuffed. We were also thoroughly exhausted—Martin and I because we had had a trying day, Coretta because she was recuperating from an operation, Juanita because she had taken care of the children, cooked, and served two meals. Martin and I made our way into the family room and collapsed into two matching love seats, our heads propped on one arm, our legs hanging over the other. I remember him saying, 'Ralph, I wish you'd had enough money to buy a whole sofa instead of just a half sofa.' Juanita overheard him and brought a pillow, which she placed under his head. I laughed and then settled more deeply into the cushion. As we talked for a few minutes, the silences grew longer. We both fell asleep. I figured we would be awakened when Juanita and Coretta finished in the kitchen, but Coretta out of the hospital only a week or two, went back to the guest bedroom to lie down, and Juanita, as usual, put her head on the kitchen counter. We all were awakened around eight the next morning when Ralph III came into the kitchen, ready for breakfast.

"It was the last evening our two families spent together.

"I hurried into the bathroom to shave. Both of us were slow starters in the morning. Together we could tie up a mirror for the better part of an hour. So even though I got a head start on Martin, I was still late for the staff meeting. As executive vice president, Andy Young had begun without us, but when I arrived he yielded the chair. Upon Martin's arrival, he sat in the back of the room and quietly observed the meeting. After a few minutes, I yielded the meeting to Martin. The chief item on the agenda was the Poor People's Campaign.

"All day Monday I waited in Atlanta for Martin to call from Washington, but I didn't hear from him until Tuesday in the middle of the afternoon. 'Hello, David,' he said casually. 'How

are you doing? Please, let's not go till tomorrow.' I heard the plaintive quality in his voice. 'OK,' I said, 'we'll go tomorrow.' So we waited till Wednesday. I drove over to his house and he was still back in his bedroom stuffing his briefcase with books. Coretta came in and we both helped Martin pack—I had to break the speed limit to make the plane, pushing my 1955 Ford to its capacity. It was a short flight to Memphis, but we sat on the runway for more than an hour. Finally, the pilot broke the silence. 'Ladies and gentlemen,' he said, 'we have a celebrity on the plane and we had a bomb threat. Though we guarded the aircraft all night, we were still required to check every piece of luggage. That's why we've been delayed. Now we're cleared for takeoff.' Martin chuckled. He was embarrassed and said 'Ralph

why would they tell me that . . . if they are going to kill me, why do it like that?' He was very nervous when we arrived in Memphis. Seldom was he relaxed.

"Juanita and I had been out of the country, on a world trip for peace, during the month of January, and Martin and Coretta took care of our children. When I returned, Martin was a totally new individual. A different individual. He wanted me to understand everything that had taken place while I was away, he wanted me to understand every sermon that he had preached. He had preached his 'Drum Major for Justice' sermon. 'If anybody is around when my day comes, don't preach a long sermon, just say that I tried to help somebody that I tried to love somebody'

Our flight had landed just ahead of bad weather, and outside the motel we could hear the wind whipping against the glass window and see flashes of lightning. By 4:30 it was dark. Later, after eating, we held a meeting in our motel suite, but nothing much was decided. Then someone reminded Martin that he was scheduled to speak that night. I could see his face lighten up. Martin looked at me. 'Ralph, I want you to go and speak for me tonight.' I hesitated. I knew that the people, however few, would be deeply disappointed to hear a substitute. 'Why don't you let Jesse go?' I suggested. 'He loves to speak.' Martin brushed the suggestion aside. 'Nobody else can speak for me. I want you to go.'

As I stepped in the door, a crowd of TV cameramen converged on me while flashbulbs exploded. I counted seven or eight television cameras already set in place. The networks were there, as well as the Memphis channels. That meant the audience would be national, so the event was much more important. I stood there for a second, then made up my mind. Turning to a technician, I asked if there was a telephone in the building. 'What do you want with a telephone?' Jesse asked. 'I'm going to call Martin.' I called the Lorraine Motel and he seemed to be in a slightly better mood. 'Martin,' I said, 'all the television networks are lined up, waiting for you. This speech will be broadcast nationwide. You need to deliver it. Besides, the people who are here want you, not me.' He responded so readily that I was surprised. 'OK, I'll come.' 'Martin,' I said. 'Don't you fool me now. You are coming, aren't you?' 'David,' he said, 'did I ever tell you I'd do something and then not come through?'

Room at the Lorraine Motel.

I heard a sudden cheer followed by applause and turned to see Martin coming down the aisle. They were standing now and, though there were only five hundred of them, they sounded like several thousand. Martin came up on the stage, acknowledged the crowd, then sat down beside me. The presiding officer turned to us. 'Which one of you wants to go first?' Martin had always spoken first, providing the inspiration. Then I followed with a practical discussion of tactics and logistics. But tonight I was inexplicably moved to alter that sequence. 'Let me go first,' I said. Martin raised an eyebrow, but nodded. He figured I must have had a reason. But in fact, I had no reason, just an impulse. I wanted to talk about Martin, my dearest friend. And for the first time I did. In doing so I was trying to sum up the greatness of the man in a way I had never done before. I don't think he quite understood my motives, and I'm not sure even now I understand fully myself. But when I finally gave him to the audience they went wild.

"He turned with a grin on his face and said, 'You took a terribly long time to introduce me.' He turned quickly to the crowd and said, 'I want everybody to know that my dearest friend in the world is Ralph Abernathy.' When he addressed the audience he was at the height of his powers. I never saw him better. Then he went into that strangely prophetic finale that still haunts me and the memory of America:

"'Well, I don't know what will happen now. We've got some difficult days ahead. But it really doesn't matter with me now, because I've been to *the mountaintop*. And I don't mind. Like anybody, I would like to live a long life. Longevity has its place. But I'm not concerned about that now. I just want to do God's will. And he's allowed me to go up to the mountain, and I've looked over, and *I've seen the promised land*. I may not get there with you. But I want you to know tonight that we as a people will get to the promised land. And so I'm happy tonight. I'm not worried about anything. I'm not fearing any man. *Mine eyes have seen the glory of the coming of the Lord.*'

"Emotionally drained, Martin's eyes were filled with tears."

—RDA

THE MEMPHIS MARCH

On Monday, April 8, we were invited back to Memphis to finally march nonviolently through the streets in honor of Martin and for the sanitation workers' strike, but actually it was the first march in honor of Martin Luther King Jr., now a legend. Sen. Ted Kennedy came to join the 100,000 marchers. In death, Martin was victorious, although our souls were heavy with grief.

(Opposite) Yolanda, Martin III, Dexter, Coretta, Ralph, Hosea Williams, Donzaleigh (with head bowed), and Andrea Young.

The first viewing at Hanley Bell Street Funeral Home: (from left to right) Yolanda, Bernice, Robert Williams, Martin III, Dexter, Aunt Coretta, Dora McDonald (Martin's secretary), and Ralph III. I was the last person at that viewing to see the body because I was afraid and I sat in the second row crying until everyone passed. Then my father took me to see Uncle Martin for the last time. He was the first person I loved who died.

Deacon H. C. Clemons walks with Martin Luther King Sr. as he views his son's body at Sister's Chapel, Spellman College.

The funeral.

RESURRECTION OF THE PEOPLE
The Courage to Walk Alone

Beams of heaven as I go through this wilderness below. Guide my feet in peaceful ways, turn my midnights into days; when in darkness I would roam, faith always sees a star of hope and soon from all life's grief and danger, I shall be free someday. Harder yet may be the fight. Right may often yield to might. Wickedness a while may reign . . .

There is a God that rules above with hand of power and heart of love. If I am right, he'll fight my battles, I shall have peace someday. The course I do not know how long 'twill be, nor what the future holds for me, but this I know, if Jesus leads me, I shall get home someday.

—C. A. Tindley

room and check on my Daddy; sometimes I would sit just to hear him snore.

It wouldn't be until years later, when I was older, that I was sure that Martin wouldn't take Daddy in the night. His grief could not last, because time healed the immediacy of his wounds. Love is the only lasting thing in the universe.

There was a struggle in the black community that finally summoned Ralph from his silence. Juanita pleaded with him to let the Movement go, but he reminded her of the promise he had made to Martin. Emerging from his vacuum of sadness, he mounted the "Poor People's Campaign." Yet he was unable to find anyone to fill the void left by Martin's passing. His only comfort was during the quiet times spent reminiscing with A.D. (Martin's brother). This abruptly ended in July 1969 when A.D. tragically drowned in his swimming pool. So Ralph walked alone, guided by faith and the will to serve, until his journey's end on April 17, 1990.

In the days following Martin's burial, sadness and grief overwhelmed Ralph. For the first time I saw a lonely man, who often sat alone in the darkness. There was nothing that Juanita or any one could do to console him. Martin was gone and had taken part of Ralph's spirit with him. I kept hoping and praying that his grief would not last. If life was not forever, then perhaps grief too was not forever. Gently, I would knock on his bedroom door, hoping to have a moment with him, hoping that I might do or say something outrageous enough to make him laugh. He wouldn't answer. If I was delivering food, I would tiptoe into the room, place the tray of food on the bench at the foot of the bed beside his chair, and ask, "Is there anything I can get for you, Daddy?" He would politely decline in a whisper and I would quietly exit, taking the previous plate of untouched food from an earlier meal. I didn't know what to say or do. I was afraid that the ghost of Martin would return and take the rest of Daddy. During those late hours, I would rise from my bed, go to my parents'

He said, "They were ordinary men put in an extraordinary circumstance, and they rose with courage to the occasion." He did not serve for money, nor for fame, but for people and for his friend." All those years, Ralph and Martin were never paid for working in the Movement. Ralph didn't think it was morally right to profit from the suffering and injustices inflicted upon black and poor people. We lived from his salary as a pastor and his speaking engagements. When "Granddaddy" King and Coretta wanted to move Martin's body from the cemetery, Ralph gave them the funds from his dwindling Southern Christian Leadership Conference (SCLC) treasury to purchase the land between Ebenezer Baptist Church and the soon-to-be-erected King Center for Martin's final resting place. Whatever we needed he said God would provide. Then he would quote Luke 12:27 "Consider the lilies . . . Solomon in all his glory was not arrayed like one of these. Have faith.

(Above) A.D., Andy, and Ralph in Washington.

(Top) Ralph's fight for school lunch programs for children.

(Above) Native Americans, Mexican Americans, and Ralph.

(Top) Resurrection City.

The Poor People's Campaign

After the death of Martin Luther King Jr., Ralph David Abernathy took over the leadership of the Poor People's Campaign, which they had created together. The Poor People's Campaign was designed to bring together groups of poor people from all over America to petition the government to create programs and policies that would respond to the needs of the poor and the disenfranchised. The poor had always been ignored politically, powerless, ostracized, and invisible to the remainder of society. The majority of black, Latino, and Native American people were poor, and the majority of poor people in America were white. This was common ground upon which to unite us. The primary objective of the campaign was to publicize their plight and place the issue of poverty in America squarely before the eyes of the nation. In the Poor People's Campaign, the poor from all walks of life came together as one people. Latin Americans from the southwest, African Americans from the rural South and urban North, white Americans from Appalachia, Native Americans from the Indian reservations, and Puerto Ricans from the eastern seaboard moved across the country and converged on Washington, D.C. On May 13, 1968, nearly 5,000 people set up residence

(Above) Bernard and Ralph promote the needs of poor people.

(Top) Marlon Brando and the Black Panthers.

(Above) Ralph and Jesse at Resurrection City Hall.

(Top) John Adams and Ralph in a wagon.

in an encampment on the Mall of the Lincoln Memorial called Resurrection City. In order to live in Resurrection City each participant had to register and sign "Pledges of Nonviolence." Their housing on the Mall was plywood A-frame structures with plastic doorways to keep out the rain. Every day combined delegations from each of the different groups went into negotiations with congressional representatives and government officials with the immediate goal of bringing attention to the plight of the poor. Because of the continuous rain and deteriorating living conditions, the government was forced to take notice of the muddy wooden settlement.

During these days, the majority of black and Latin people were poor, and the majority of poor people in America were white. This reality was common ground upon which we could all be united. Around the country, the poor were dramatizing their plight with escalating acts of violence. This rage grew from the desperate seeds of bitterness, empty promises, hopelessness, and years of neglect. This matter of poverty was an urgent one and could not be postponed by political posturing. The escalating violence stemmed from the disgust that festered in the hearts of these men because their living conditions and the chances to improve them were far below the nation's average

The anniversary of Martin's birthday is always a bitter-sweet occasion for me, because I remember a life of courage and glory and also one cut short by mindless hatred. This year, controversy surrounding my autobiography *And the Walls Came Tumbling Down* has made this my most trying year since 1968. I wrote to let future generations know what it was like to be on the front lines of the Civil Rights Movement—so they could know and love the real Martin Luther King—the warm, caring, and at times humorous man whose courage and vision redeemed a nation. No one knew Martin better than I did, or had the closeness of the friendship Martin and I shared . . . my deep and obvious admiration for him has given a sympathetic portrait of his life and character.

"The *Washington Post* said, 'Abernathy's own life story is the closest that researchers and students will ever get to a full autobiography of King, its loving depiction of the true friendship between Abernathy and King . . .' I have written of my dearest friend. For almost 15 years we were inseparable, not only because we were joined together in a great struggle to free our people, but also because we loved each other like brothers. When he went to jail, I went with him. (Most of the time we shared the same cell.) When he marched in Birmingham and Selma and Chicago, I marched beside him. When he faced the dogs and the tear gas, I faced them too. When he worried over a problem at some cheap motel in a strange and hostile city, I worried with him. And when he was gunned down in Memphis, I was the one who rode with him in the ambulance; and after the doctors had given up on him, it was I, and I alone, who cradled him in my arms until he died.

"Martin Luther King Jr. was not just a great public hero but an extremely attractive human being as well—a man whom you would have loved to have as a friend. Most people remember the eloquent but solemn preacher who became the conscience of an entire generation. Or they see the grim-faced leader marching at the head of a civil rights army. And surely this was one part of Martin—the public man. But I want to show the private man as well: the mimic who was so funny he could render his friends helpless with laughter; the young sol-dier who loved life and was afraid to die, but went into battle anyway; the great leader who on the last day of his life worried about hurting the feelings of a tired waitress who had brought the wrong order. I want my readers to see the man I remembered and love in all his humanity.

"First J. Edgar Hoover, and later enemies of Dr. King, attempted to exploit our weakness to disable the Movement. I have written my own recollections to add to the body of knowledge about the most dramatic events in modern America and about the century's greatest hero. These critics quarreling about the past have forgotten about the problems we face in the present. We have come a long way. It's a tribute to our great movement and democracy that blacks served as mayors, congressmen, and the governor of a Southern state. Leadership addresses the problems that still face our people: poverty, homelessness, illiteracy, black-on-black crime, teenage pregnancy, drug abuse. Many are more concerned with making millions than with helping millions, worried about image status and spending their time in front of television cameras.

"We must now turn our attention to those who have been left behind in the dust of our past victories. For there are countless numbers of hopeless children trapped in inner cities, hooked on drugs, robbing and assaulting their own people, not only victims but also creators of despair . . . do something about those children! Provide them with strong leaders! Help them stay in school, stay off drugs, and stay out of jail! Prepare uneducated and unskilled blacks to fill their share of the new technological jobs our society is daily creating. March again—for economic opportunity and for programs that will transform our inner cities from battlegrounds into peaceful, prosperous communities. Most of all, believe in yourselves the way we did in Montgomery, Birmingham, and Selma, when the Civil Rights Movement gave us dignity and purpose as a people, when we were led by Martin Luther King Jr."

—RDA
January 15, 1990

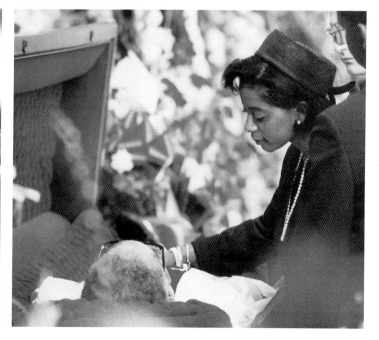

SAYING GOOD-BYE TO MY FATHER

On the morning of Friday, March 23, 1990, the telephone rang in my Santa Monica bungalow at the beach. Through my exhaustion I heard my father's voice saying, "Hello, darling, this is Daddy." He called that morning as he had done so many mornings before. Only this morning was different. I could hear hesitation in his voice. Usually he was playful and deliberate about waking me. This particular morning, he was quiet and introspective. He asked about my life, then spoke about his spiritual fast and the weight that he had lost. Then, from what appeared to be out of nowhere, he said, "I just called to say, my dear . . . I'm sorry . . . for not being there for you all the years of your childhood. You were not the most important thing in my life then. It was the Movement. You were second and I'm so sorry." He took a long pause. "I'm sorry that I missed the joy of watching you grow up. But your mother has done a tremendous job in raising you. You are a fine young woman." My eyes grew wet with tears. He had never said these words to me before, or apologized to me for the time he had spent away on the road. Didn't he know how much he had given me? He had given me the freedom to be who and what I wanted to be in the world. Freedom that allowed me to live how I wanted with whom I wanted, where I wanted. He meant everything to me. It was no secret in my family that I was in awe of my father. For over an hour we spoke that morning, cherishing our memories. Then he said good-bye and gave me his best wishes for a happy life. When we hung up, my heart sank.

Later that evening, after returning from a film screening at the Director's Guild of America, I played my messages on the answering machine. My brother, Ralph III, had called. Daddy had collapsed, become unconscious, and was taken to the hospital. Before his collapse he kept telling Mother, "It's over, it's over. . . . It's all over." Dewey and Mardell Duncan were visiting from out of town, so Mother was not alone to care for Daddy. His body had shut down because it had been depleted of salt, and the paramedics had to revive him. My brother begged, "Please come." I saw the night end and the morning begin from my seat by the window as I flew across the sky. The whole of my life flashed before my eyes and the memories of my youth engulfed me. The last time I had seen my father was a few months earlier, as we sat together in the San Diego airport waiting for his plane to Atlanta. I asked him, "Daddy, what will I do when you are gone?" He replied, "Live, Donzaleigh, live. Grieve for a moment, but remember, life goes on." I leaned my head on his shoulder as we sat in silence. "It's not fair," I said. "Your life has been so hard." Then he said, "Must Jesus bear the cross alone and all the world go free? No. There's a cross for everyone and this is the cross for me."

Months earlier we celebrated Christmas together. We went as a family to my sister's home in Germany, as we had done on so many previous holidays. Juandalynn lived in Konstanz at a resort on a lake that bordered Switzerland. My cousin Vivian even came up from her home in Greece. Daddy rested a lot, and we showered him with constant affection. After New Year's, my younger brother, Kwame, had to return to Williams College in Massachusetts where he was in the middle of his freshman year. So Daddy took him back to America, and we set off to Istanbul to explore the religious world of Turkey.

Three months later, I found myself walking into Emory University's Crawford Long Hospital to say good-bye to my father for the last time. When I arrived that morning, he was alert, watching everything but saying nothing. Suddenly the door opened and a team of doctors and nurses burst into the room and asked me to leave: "Visitors are not allowed this early." In all the commotion I felt a hand shoving me away. As they closed the door in my face, I heard my father's powerful voice ring out like it did on Sunday mornings: "Donzaleigh, my child." It shocked everyone in the room because they had only heard Daddy's silence. I answered my father, entered the room, and took my position at the head of the bed beside him. My brother made the necessary introductions and from that moment on, my father said nothing more.

My sister came in from Europe, and over the next few weeks, Daddy progressively got better. I entertained him with my outrageous humor, in between his divinely inspired insights on life. "I'm alive!" he said. "I'm alive! I'm alive forevermore!" The depth of his spiritual wisdom was profound. He spoke about Montgomery, Glen Smiley, Al Lingo and Martin. In those last few weeks he gave us words, guidance, and knowledge to live by for the remainder of our lives. His doctors were planning to release him on April 18 to return home. On the evening of April 16, the course of events took a turn for the worse. I sat alone with Daddy, reading while he slept. He awakened and said that he felt "a fullness" in his chest. He wanted to know the date and the time. I glanced at a newspaper and gave him a date, but not owning a watch, I couldn't give him the time. So he had me look around for one of his watches, which I couldn't locate. He got up from the bed, walked around, and suddenly collapsed. Miraculously, I was by his side. With strength that I was unaware I had, I caught and held up his limp body, then gently guided him to the floor. I rang the emergency button for the nurses and a huge male nurse came to our rescue. After Daddy was placed on the bed, he regained consciousness. He continued to speak about the fullness in his chest. The nurses brought in machines that registered no activity. They sent for a doctor from the emergency room while we waited for his regular doctor to arrive. Soon Mother and Juandalynn were there. We stood around as the ER doctor tried a second machine to register the activity of my father's heart. His blood pressure was dangerously low, so it was decided that he needed to be moved to critical care for the remainder of the night. As we rolled down the corridor, he said, "I should be worried about myself now, but I'm not. I can't think about me now. I can only think about you. Juanita . . . You have to forgive them. It is the only way to make it into the Kingdom." We stood there, the women: my mother, my sister, and me.

In the twilight of the morning, he spoke about forgiveness, about others, his care, and his love . . . on the brink of death, my father, who was so great, so humble, who gave his life for humanity and asked for nothing, could only think of others.

The head nurse on the critical care watch refused to let me sleep in the room with Daddy. So, for the first time since his hospital stay, he was alone. Mother and Juandalynn returned home, and I went back to Daddy's old hospital room and fell asleep. The sun rose as I wrapped myself in Daddy's covers. A nurse came to fetch me to feed my daddy his breakfast. I raised my head, said I was coming, and fell back to sleep. She came back again to wake me and his doctor was standing there. They were going to take him down for some tests. They were afraid that he had suffered a blood clot and wanted to see where it was lodged. Nervously, I sprang from the bed and started down the hall for my daddy. Dr. Ollins followed, assuring me that everything was all right. When I got there the gurney and two nurses had arrived. My father was gasping for each breath. On his chest I could see the crumbs from his muffin and the empty tray beside him. As I watched my daddy fight for air to breathe, I was never so afraid in my life. "Let me help you," I said. "Stand back, Donzaleigh, there is nothing you can do," Daddy said. "I don't remember telling anybody this is my time to meet my Creator." He was in pain. They rolled the gurney out of the room. "I will go with you, Daddy," I said. "I will go where you go."

As a little girl I had told God that if he would spare my father's life, I would freely give mine. And if the moment were to come that God should take him, then I would go too. I never wanted to know a day when he wasn't in this world. His life had so much meaning. He knew that morning what I wanted. He always understood me. "You can't go where I've got to go, Donzaleigh." Then he told me to go pack up the

EPILOGUE

A lot has occurred in the world since the days of the Civil Right Movement. Our society is more integrated, yet our neighborhoods are still segregated. Our children continue to be educated in schools that are barely integrated and, unlike during the days of the Civil Rights Movement, children have taken up arms and are killing each other in random, senseless acts of violence, as evidenced by the tragic events at Columbine. Racial discord following the Rodney King verdict destroyed sections of Los Angeles, and racial tension escalated after the Nicole Brown Simpson and Ron Goldman murder trial, helping to further divide the nation. President William Jefferson Clinton and his administration worked to restore racial harmony and provide economic prosperity. However, internationally, America's domestic policies and affluence were taking prominence on the world stage.

Affirmative action, which ensured fair educational and employment opportunities for all people of color and women, was eliminated in California, where the majority of the population are Latinos and females, who are still referred to as minorities. As a result, college admissions dropped significantly for non-whites at major universities in California. In Colorado and Texas, angry groups of white men victimized and killed individual black men. Random burnings of black churches, which ended in the 1960s, recurred in the nineties all over the South. Right-wing extremist Timothy McVeigh orchestrated the tragic bombing of the Federal building in Oklahoma City, killing hundreds of adults and children. H. G. Wells wrote, "The greatest evil known to man is racial hatred," and hatred would eventually become the death of society.

On September 11, 2001, people all over the world cried and watched in horror as the World Trade Center's Twin Towers crumbled, smoldered, and burned. Innocent lives locked inside the buildings were lost forever. Within moments, hatred killed more than 2,800 human beings and destroyed the lives of thousands more. That same hatred crashed American Airlines Flight 64 into the Pentagon in Washington, D.C., momentarily rendering America vulnerable. The lives of 125 service persons, defense employees, and con-

tract workers along with 77 innocent passengers burned in the ruin of the Pentagon. Then, in a remote region of Pennsylvania, passengers on United Airlines Flight 93 fought courageously against their captors, limiting the casualties to the 45 people on board.

For those moments the world stood still and took notice of the evil of hatred. For a brief moment, we put aside our differences, swallowed our pride, dropped our defenses, and checked in with each other. During those moments, we tried desperately to call our loved ones near and far, especially those isolated on Manhattan Island. We remembered those we had forgotten and how much we loved them. For some our only solace was looking into the faces of strangers, trying to summon courage in our hearts, as people walked silently by the thousands, covered in smoke, ash, and debris up the avenues of New York and out of the tunnels of Washington. In that moment, as more than two thousand people trapped inside those buildings were suffocating in death, survivors fought to catch their breath, while witnesses held their breath in disbelief. For those who lost loved ones, all that remains is love. Love triumphed over hatred on September 11, 2001; love of the human spirit, and the reality that life goes on. Love is not a sentimental word spoken in moments of deep emotion. Love is life's greatest and most enduring force expressed in action. Love triumphed in Washington, New York, and Pennsylvania, just as it had in Montgomery, Birmingham, and Selma. Martin Luther King said, "When you rise to love on this level, you love every man because God loves them, and love is greater than like. The dignity of the human spirit and the love of humanity are all that will remain as the memory of these heroic men and women.

The laws of nature have taught us that all species on the face of the earth over time, adapt, mutate and eventually merge together in peaceful co-existence. Therefore the hatred, religious or racial, which seems to divide humanity will not last forever. Eventually, it will be wiped out. Human beings will learn to live peacefully together or we will all perish, together. The laws of nature are greater than the will of man. If you question the laws of nature, then look at a tornado, feel the power of an earthquake, stand near the ocean in a hurricane or in the radius of the force of an erupting volcano. Man is powerless to halt the forces of nature and God. Our future lies in our love and acceptance of one another, conquering our fears and disillusionments about our differences. We are all the same, human beings. Integration, compassion and understanding for our fellow man are the answers. I am a living witness to the power of love and its effects upon humanity. One day future generations will know the truth that I speak. "Men will beat their swords into plowshares, their spears into pruning hooks, and study war no more, thus saith the Lord."

I hope that this book of remembrance will give guidance to you, as it has given me. It has been a long journey to completion. But my greatest joy through this process has been to keep my father alive and present in my life. This journey all began for me in 1990, shortly after my father's death, while I was visiting Robert Kennedy Jr. As Bobby shared with me the book he had written about his dear friend whom I had the great pleasure of knowing, I knew that I too had to write. It was right that only Bobby should write the foreword to this book. It has taken much time to bring this book to the public. But as my father always taught me, "The battle is not to the swift nor the strong, but to he who endureth to the end." My father, whom I called "Reverend" because of his sincere faith in and service to God, said, "Freedom is not simply the right to do as you please. Freedom is when it pleases you to do what is right." I have tried to do what is right. Peace.

ACKNOWLEDGMENTS

Crown/Random House: Chris Jackson, my editor, and the marketing, art, and sales departments.

GPG: Quay Hays, Peter Hoffman, Dominic Friesen, Susan Landesmann, Robert Avellan, Susan Anson, Rene Ridinger, and Harlan Boll.

Victoria Sanders, my agent at VSA.

Legal: Jay Cooper and Rose Scaraglino of Greenberg-Traurig, and Carl Grumer of Manatt, Phelps & Phillips.

Technical support: Planet Blue

Web design: Joel Ashman

Publicity and promotions: Ginnina D'Orazio

Personal assistance: Christopher Stark, Jonathan Tamarkin, Brenda Jean Bakke, Suzanna Preston, Ivy Simmons, Roby Pettit, and Anna Cabo.

My family: Mother, Juandalynn, Ralph III, Kwame Luthuli, Ralph IV, Christiana, Micah, and Soren-Niklas, for whom I tell this story. Our loved ones: Annette Williams Abernathy and Sven-Torben Haderup.

The King family: Aunt Coretta, Yolanda, Martin III, Dexter, and Bernice.

Bobby Kennedy Jr., for your friendship, support, and foreword.

Marilynn Young, for traveling with me to New York at the beginning of this endeavor and introducing me to the following historic photographic archives: Associated Press, Corbis, The Library of Congress, Black Star, Magnum, and Panopticon.

Elaine Tomlin, the SCLC staff photographer, who taught me about the art of photography.

Dan Budnik, Matt Herron, Charles Moore, and Ernest Withers, for sharing with me their candid photography.

Special thanks to:
Holly Jones and Ann Perkins of AP; Sally of Magnum; Amy Rennert of Gilbertson/Kincaid; JoAn, Gordon, and Ron; Merritt and Rick of The Blake Agency; Ron Maxwell of Gods and Generals; The *Any Day Now* cast and crew; and Dr. Noel Brown and Irving Sarnoff of Friends of the United Nations.

Personal thanks to:
Comarletia Harris Pierce, Temple, Kate and Otis Richardson, Grandma Josephine Brown, Christopher N., Krista Errickson and Piero di Pasquale, Paivi Hartzell and Jukka Kemppinnen, Heather Schmidt and Bob Wiswall, Dr. Dorothy Yancy, Janet Smith, Nan Richardson and John Richardson, Dar B., Miss Kim, young Amanda Goodman, and all the wonderful students I have met while visiting schools. And Purcella, my childhood friend who taught me about her Hawaiian/Chinese heritage.

During research:
New York—Bob and Jean Abernathy Evans, Kevin and Jenna Davis, Geoffrey and Carol Kirshner, Anthony D. Parrish, Eileen Tasca, and Robin and Larry Valenza. Washington/Maryland—Tiffany and the McMillan family, Erica Jones, and Rudy and Athalee Abernathy-Anderson.

Thank you to all the peaceful warriors of the Civil Rights Movement who gave their lives for the greater good of humanity, especially Rosa, Glenn, Uncle Martin, and Daddy. Thank you for entrusting me with this wonderful legacy.

Thank you God for my life.

BIBLIOGRAPHY

Abernathy, Ralph David. 1989. *And the Walls Came Tumbling Down.* New York: Harper & Row.

———. 1958. *The Natural History of a Social Movement.* Master's thesis, Atlanta University.

The American Negro as a Politician. 1966. Atlanta: Southern Christian Leadership Conference Publishers.

Branch, Taylor. 1989. *Parting the Waters: America in the King Years, 1954–1963.* New York: Touchstone Books.

The Broadman Hymnal. 1940. Nashville: Broadman Press.

Couto, Richard A. 1994. *Ain't Gonna Let Nobody Turn Me Around: The Pursuit of Racial Justice in the Rural South.* Philadelphia: Temple University Press.

Farina, Richard. 1964. *Birmingham Sunday.* New York: Ryerson Music Publishers, Inc.

Garrow, David J. 1986. *Bearing the Cross.* New York: First Vintage Books.

———. 1989. *The Walking City: The Montgomery Bus Boycott, 1955–56.* Brooklyn: Carlson Publishing, Inc.

Harkinswheat, Ellen. 1991. *Jacob Lawrence: The Frederick Douglass and Harriet Tubman Series of 1938–1940.* Seattle: University of Washington Press.

Kasher, Steven. 1995. *The Civil Rights Movement.* New York: Abbeville Press.

King, Martin Luther, Jr. 1963. *Strength to Love.* New York: Harper & Row.

———. 1963. *Why We Can't Wait.* New York: Signet and Mentor Books.

———. 1968. *The Wisdom of Martin Luther King: In His Own Words.* Mt. Ida, Ariz.: Lancer Books.

Lancer, Brian, and Barbara Summers. 1989. *I Dream a World: Portraits of Black Women Who Changed America.* New York: Stewart, Tabori & Chang.

Long, Richard A. 1989. *The Black Tradition in American Dance.* New York: Multimedia Books.

Pepper, William F. 1995. *Orders to Kill.* New York: Warner Books.

PHOTO CREDITS

page 188
(top) Bob Fitch, Black Star;
(bottom) Vernon Merritt III, Black
Star
page 189
AP/Wide World Photos
page 190
John C. Goodwin
page 191
(top) AP/Wide World Photos;
(bottom) John C. Goodwin
page 192
AP/Wide World Photos
page 193
AP/Wide World Photos
page 194
(all photos) AP/Wide World Photos
page 195
The Abernathy Family Collection
page 196
(top right, center) The Abernathy
Family Collection; (bottom left)
Scott L. Henderson; (bottom right)
Ivan Massar, Black Star; (bottom)
Black Star

page 198
The Abernathy Family Collection
page 199
UPI/Corbis
page 200
The Abernathy Family Collection
page 202
The Abernathy Family Collection
page 203
UPI/Corbis
page 204
(top) Costa Manos, Magnum Photos
© 1968; (bottom) AP/Wide World
Photos
page 205
UPI/Corbis
page 206
(top) AP/Wide World Photos;
(bottom) Flip Schulke, Black Star
page 207
AP/Wide World Photos
page 208
The Abernathy Family Collection
page 209
I. Henry Phillips, The Afro-American
file photo

page 210
(bottom right) Owen, Black Star;
(all other photos) Bob Fitch, Black
Star
page 211
(top) C. J. Fax, Black Star; (bottom
left) Mike Mauney, Black Star;
(bottom right) Flip Schulke, Black
Star
pages 212–213
The Abernathy Family Collection
pages 214–215
The Abernathy Family Collection
page 216
(top left) AP/Wide World Photos;
(bottom left) Elaine Tomlin, The
Abernathy Family Collection; (right)
Elaine Tomlin, SCLC file photo
page 217
SCLC file photo, Boston Chapter
page 218
top row: (left) UPI/Corbis; (right)
The Abernathy Family Collection
bottom row: (left and right)
UPI/Corbis

page 219
top row: (left and right) UPI/Corbis
bottom row: (left) The Abernathy
Family Collection; (right) AP/Wide
World Photos
page 223
first row: (left) AP/Wide World
Photos; (right) UPI/Corbis
second row: (left) The Abernathy
Family Collection; (right) AP/Wide
World Photos
third row: (left) Al Noriega,
Bakersfield College file photo;
(right) UPI/Corbis
fourth row: (left and right) AP/Wide
World Photos
page 225
(top) The Abernathy Family
Collection; (bottom left and right)
AP/Wide World Photos
page 230
Elaine Tomlin, The Abernathy Family
Collection

INDEX